T0312762

THE ACCOUNTING HALL OF FAME

The Ohio State University

Thomas J. Burns Series in Accounting History

VOLUME 3
James L. Peirce: A Collection of His Writings

James L. Peirce
1907 – 1994

JAMES L. PEIRCE
A Collection of His Writings

Edited by

Edward N. Coffman
Virginia Commonwealth University

Daniel L. Jensen
The Ohio State University

The Accounting Hall of Fame
THE OHIO STATE UNIVERSITY
Max M. Fisher College of Business
1997

Manufactured in the United States of America
Printed on acid-free paper

ISBN 1-883356-03-1

TABLE OF CONTENTS

EDITORS' PREFACE

This volume brings together the writings of Mr. James L. Peirce in recognition of his contributions to the profession of accounting. Through the years, many individuals have made significant contributions to the growth and development of the accounting profession. Fifty-eight such individuals, including James L. Peirce, have been elected to The Accounting Hall of Fame at The Ohio State University since the Hall was established in 1950. The scholarly contributions of some of these important accountants—particularly those in academe—have been collected and published in special volumes, as a way of documenting and preserving a written record of contributions. But the contributions of many others remain dispersed in difficult to access periodicals, books, and manuscripts. These are in danger of being forgotten. The record of contributions by accountants who, like James L. Peirce, made their careers outside academe are particularly vulnerable to being lost.

This volume is the third in a series presenting the collected works of Hall of Fame members whose works have not been collected and published elsewhere. This series was established in 1992 in recognition of the quarter century of administrative service to The Accounting Hall of Fame by Thomas J. Burns (1923-1996).

A chronological bibliography of Mr. Peirce's writings and speeches appears at the end of this volume. The bibliography includes the writings and speeches that we were able to locate through searches of bibliographic sources including *The Accountants' Index* as prepared by the American Institute of Certified Public Accountants. Copies of all items in our bibliography were located.

In selecting the works to appear in this volume, we have attempted to present items that reveal Mr. Peirce's views on accounting and controllership as practiced in the private sector. We have attempted to minimize redundancy by reproducing just one version of similar papers or speeches. The editors' footnote to each item identifies the source of the item reproduced and cites duplicate or nearly duplicate items that are omitted from the collection.

We have endeavored to reproduce Mr. Peirce's writings as they originally appeared. Published materials are reproduced using Mr. Peirce's complete text; however, some editorial and stylistic elements of the journal are omitted in the interests of a uniform style. Occasionally, we have made comments and explanations in footnotes to the articles and speeches reproduced here. These are identified as "editors' notes" and printed in italics.

Mr. Peirce's works are arranged in three groups of related articles: (1) controllership and the control process, (2) budgets: principles of human relationship, and (3) emergence of the financial executive. The groups are presented in an order that preserves their approximate chronology as the best means of tracing the development of his thinking and philosophy.

We are grateful to the Thomas J. Burns Trust, the Department of Accounting and Management Information Systems at The Ohio State University, and the Department of Accounting at Virginia Commonwealth University for supporting this project. We are also grateful for the invaluable assistance of Barbara Eide, doctoral candidate at Virginia Commonwealth University. Finally we wish to acknowledge the Canadian Institute of Chartered Accountants, Financial Executives Institute, Harvard Business School, and the Illinois Manufacturers' Association for permission to reproduce Mr. Peirce's writings in this volume.

August 1997   Edward N. Coffman
                                        Virginia Commonwealth University

                                        Daniel L. Jensen
                                        The Ohio State University

A BIOGRAPHY
of
JAMES L. PEIRCE

James Loring Peirce, the son of Loring Hampton and Rose Drago Peirce, was born on September 13, 1907, in Valparaiso, Indiana.[1] Upon the death of his father, Peirce and his mother moved to Chicago where he graduated from Nicholas Senn High School in 1924. His first employment was with The Union Trust Company, which later became part of the First National Bank of Chicago. It was here that his interest in the field of finance began. While pursuing his professional career, he attended evening classes at Northwestern University, graduating in 1930. Peirce was very active on campus serving as class president, editor of the school's business magazine, and president of Northwestern's chapter of Alpha Kappa Psi. He received the Delta Sigma Pi Award for scholarship and campus activities.[2] In 1932, he was certified as a CPA in Illinois. He was married February 12, 1938 to Marion Low Field; they had two children.

In 1927, Peirce accepted a position on the Controller's staff at The Celotex Company, a Chicago-based insulation manufacturer. He left The Celotex Company in 1934 and joined A. B. Dick Company, a family-owned office equipment manufacturer, headquartered in Chicago. After serving in a number of finance-related positions, he was appointed assistant controller and designated acting controller in 1941. In 1947, he became controller, and in 1951 was named vice president-finance. He was elected a member of the Board of Directors in 1966,[3] and six years later became vice chairman, a position he held until his retirement from A. B. Dick Company in 1979. During the period of his affiliation with A. B. Dick Company, the company grew into international scope, primarily in the areas of office duplicating and copying, and later in the fields of non-impact printing and word processing.

In 1941, Peirce began a long and distinguished career with the Controllers Institute of America (now the Financial Executives Institute).[4]

---

[1]This biographical profile builds upon information contained in Thomas J. Burns and Edward N. Coffman, eds., *The Accounting Hall of Fame: Profiles of Fifty Members*, (Columbus, OH: College of Business, The Ohio State University, 1991).

[2]"James L. Peirce," Obituaries, *Evanston Review* (March 17, 1994), pp. 161, 163.

[3]"A.B. Dick Names Two Directors," *The New York Times* (August 6, 1966), p. 35.

[4]In 1962 the name was changed to the Financial Executives Institute.

He was president of the Chicago chapter in 1950. In 1953, he became a member of the National Board of Directors and remained on the Board until 1961. During this period he served as chairman of the Planning Committee (1952-53), vice president of Region VIII (1954-55), and chairman of the Second Joint Committee on Long-Range Research Objectives (1956). In 1957, he was elected national president[5] and the following year became chairman of the Board of Directors, and in 1959 chairman of the Executive Committee. As a result of the numerous activities performed for the benefit of the Institute, he was elected an honorary member of the FEI in 1959. From 1959 to 1965, he served as a trustee of the Financial Executives Research Foundation.

As a member of the FEI's International Liaison Committee he became interested in the early phases of development of financial executive groups in other countries. In 1967, he represented the FEI as a delegate and speaker at the Ninth International Congress of Accountants held in Paris. In 1969, he was keynote speaker at the First International Congress of Institutes of Financial Executives in Marbella, Spain.

In the years 1952 to 1968, Peirce authored over a dozen widely read articles on controllership, planning and control, budgeting, and related management accounting subjects. Peirce's writing was influenced by his active involvement with the Institute and his personal experience as a controller for a large company. Numerous articles focused on elevating the function of the controller from that of a chief accounting officer to a level of management participation in every phase of business decision-making based on the planning and control process. Central to Peirce's early articles were the six functions of controllership developed by the Controllers Institute's Committee on Ethics and Eligibility Standards and approved by the National Board of Directors on September 25, 1949.[6] In theory and practice, he expounded that the element of "control" in the controller's corporate title be taken literally, though carefully defined to avoid confusion with direct management authority.

In addition to advocating a modern concept of controllership, Peirce was an early advocate of a behavioral approach to budgeting. He argued that "the budget rested on principles that had more in common with concepts of human relationship than with rules of accounting."[7] Lee D. Parker identified Peirce's early contribution to this subject indicating that "Peirce indulged in a more detailed treatment of the subject than his contemporaries and even

---

[5]"Controllers Institute Chooses New President," *The New York Times* (May 17, 1957), p. 37.

[6]The six functions of controllership are reproduced in Exhibit 1 on page 18 of this volume.

[7]James L. Peirce, "The Budget Comes of Age," *Harvard Business Review* 32 (May-June 1954), p. 58.

then went beyond their limited recognitions of behavioural problems in budgeting to consider potential solutions."[8] For his many contributions to the accounting profession, including his pioneering efforts in the development of the controllership function, James L. Peirce was inducted into the Accounting Hall of Fame in 1965.

James L. Peirce is remembered for a long and distinguished career in business and public service. He had affiliations with a number of other professional and educational interests; these included the Council of Financial Executives of The Conference Board, the Economic Club of Chicago, the Union League of Chicago, and Alpha Kappa Psi. He died March 9, 1994, at the age of 86.

---

[8]Lee D. Parker, "The Behavioural Impact of Budgets: Early Accounting Contributions," *The Accounting Historians Journal* 11 (Spring 1984), p. 122.

CONTROLLERSHIP AND THE CONTROL PROCESS

THE CONTROLLERSHIP FUNCTION: A MODERN CONCEPT †

by

James L. Peirce

WHENEVER the subject of the controllership function is discussed, I am beset with the thought that, properly speaking, controllership is not a function at all. It is rather an attitude of mind. It is a presence, if you will, which enriches and vitalizes the activities of any company in which it is found. A mere set of functions may be assigned to any qualified person, but controllership goes far deeper. It is a trained viewpoint which, when properly exercised, brings balance to management thinking, escorting it through sound channels of business judgment and ushering it into the realm of profitable operation.

Let us consider, then, a modern concept, and leave yesterday's model behind. We have been accustomed for a long time to think of the controller as that executive who concerns himself with his company's accounting, costs, auditing, taxes, budgets, financial forecasts, insurance, statistics and so on. Little by little, this view has shifted to higher altitudes, until the activities of the controller have become a recognized segment of managerial thought, entering into every significant move and decision.

This trail has been pioneered by strong men. Looking backward, we can visualize them fighting through a wilderness of tradition and skepticism to win recognition of the controller as far more than an executive accountant—to carve out a new role in management. We can also recall some of the mistakes made on the way—the men who unwittingly became known for saying no to all new ideas—the men who prepared their company's budgets single-handed and then tried to enforce them—the men who tried to mix the practice of controllership with major operating duties. By these mistakes we have learned and are still learning what controllership really means.

Nor do I feel that the profit motive, as that term is generally used, is the sole impulsion of controllership, or even of business as a whole. Profits are indispensable, of course, and because the enlightened use of the profit motive

†Presented at the Conference on Controllership, jointly sponsored by the School of Business, University of Chicago, and the Chicago Control of the Controllers Institute of America. Reprinted from *The Controller*, September 1952, pp. 419-422, 428, 430-432, 434, copyright 1952, with permission of the Financial Executives Institute, 10 Madison Avenue, P.O. Box 1938, Morristown, NJ 07962-1938. (201) 898-4600.

has not usually conflicted with the attainment of other legitimate objectives, it has been a serviceable guide in making decisions. Nevertheless, it sometimes becomes necessary to sacrifice immediate profit in favor of, let us say, a long-range development program. Profits may have to yield precedence to a position more acceptable to employees and public, or even to just plain conformity to the standard of business morality that the individual management must live with because it is constituted that way. Controllership should be responsive to these finer shadings of purpose. It must never permit itself to be thought of as that element in the organization which is only capable of thinking in terms of dollars and cents. All of this is a part of an atmosphere which surrounds controllership as it must be practiced if it is to succeed.

There is a very descriptive term, originated I believe by the personnel people, which applies here very well. The term is "service motivated" and it fits that kind of man or woman we are sometimes privileged to know who, either instinctively or by self-training, places the needs of others above his own, and finds his own advancement in serving others.

The staff status of controllership demands this service motivation, and controllership finds its best expression in such a surrounding. The principles and practices of controllership cannot be separated from its ideals, and I mention this here to make clear the reason for seasoning this presentation with a liberal amount of idealism. It remains for you to judge whether these thought are also workable and practical.

CONTROLLERSHIP AND CONTROLLERS

Before launching into a description of the controllership functions, I should like to clarify what we are talking about. To understand what controllership means, it is absolutely essential to distinguish it from the office of controller as we know it from our business acquaintance.

Although the functions of controllership can best be performed by a controller, a little reflection will remind you that the assignment of controllership duties differs widely. In some companies, for instance the controller performs the accounting, cost and tax functions, while the coordination of a budgetary control program is assigned to an administrative vice president or treasurer. In other cases, the planning and control activities that are the heart of controllership are performed by staff men reporting to the president. Frequently the president or an executive vice president, does the real controllership job, leaving the man designated controller, if one exists, with a task resembling that of chief accountant.

Looking on the operating side of the fence, we sometimes find controllers carrying out assignments which are no part of controllership, such as purchasing or standards engineering. Some of them may even be found negotiating labor contracts.

Now there are usually reasons for all these heterogeneous arrangements considered valid by the managements concerned. I have no intention of criticizing them. I do, however, want to make it perfectly clear that the controller in all such cases is hampered in giving full expression to this very beneficial influence called controllership in one of two ways: either he lacks the full delegation of duties and authority to do the complete job, or he is forced to devote so much time and effort to operating tasks that he sacrifices much of the over-all planning sense and objectivity that a controller must cultivate in order to perform effectively.

The recognition of these facts need not discourage anyone. Even though the full-blown expression of the controllership idea has not been manifested in your organization through delegation of the full complement of duties to one man—even though your company is not large enough to justify a full-time controller—even though your particular job represents only one segment of the controllership field–despite the presence of one or all of these conditions in your own experience, you will profit by cultivating an understanding of the science of controllership. By understanding this science better, in all of its implications, you will practice it more effectively in those phases of controllership that fall to your execution.

Furthermore, you may be sure that if your business is profitable—if it has been even moderately successful—someone within its doors has been practicing controllership. You might find this spark of planning and control hidden deep in the thoughts of a sole owner, activated only in the hours approaching midnight, but you will find it. The captain may also be the navigator in your ship, but he cannot stay afloat without navigation.

DEFINITION OF CONTROLLERSHIP

Now that we have disposed of the confusion which is constantly arising from failure to distinguish clearly between the science of controllership and the duties assigned to individual controllers, let us turn our attention to an examination of this science as it should be practiced.

Fortunately Controllers Institute of America has hammered out—after much thought and laborious committee activity—an official statement of its concept of the function of controllership. A Chicago man was chairman of the committee which in 1949 completed this modern concept, superseding the outworn, limited sense of controllership which was generally accepted in previous years. He is E. W. Burbott, now vice chairman of A. B. Dick Company, formerly national president of Controllers Institute and subsequently president of the Controllership Foundation; and I mention him because he has made an important contribution to American business in its development of a modern concept of controllership.

Read the Institute's concept of controllership in its entirety, for this paper subsequently discusses it point by point [*see Exhibit 1, page 18*]. So much meaning has been packed into each of the six functions making up this

5

definition—so much thought given to the choice of each word—that, if you have not read it before, its full impact may not reach you with the first reading. A common first impression is that it covers an immense amount of territory. Careful thought usually makes it clear that nothing less complete will suffice. We shall analyze it and see for ourselves.

THE PLAN FOR THE CONTROL OF OPERATIONS

The first point in the Institute's statement provides a plan for the control of the operations of the business. It is the function of controllership to establish such a plan, to coordinate and maintain it. The plan must be integrated, in the sense that all departments of the business will be scheduled to move harmoniously toward a predetermined goal. Depending on the kind of business, such a plan will require, to a greater or less degree, cost standards, expense budgets, sales forecasts—all of the techniques of planning at our disposal. Even financial planning cannot be done without controllership, for current operating and long-range planning of capital requirements go hand in hand. Nor is controllership relieved of responsibility once the plan is launched. It must also provide the necessary procedures to effectuate the plan.

At this point I should like to ask you to review point one in the Institute's concept of controllership and to call your attention to three words in it—"through authorized management."

> 1. To establish, coordinate and maintain, through authorized management, an integrated plan for the control of operations. Such a plan would provide, to the extent required in the business, cost standards, expense budgets, sales forecasts, profit planning, and programs for capital investment and financing, together with the necessary procedures to effectuate the plan.

This phrase is the keynote of effective controllership. Every good controller knows—sometimes from painful experience—that he cannot move about through his organization issuing orders and instructions which will eventuate in the construction of an operating plan. If he does, it is likely that no one will follow the plan, and he will have no end of trouble in coordinating and maintaining it, because everyone will think of it as the controller's plan, rather than as the company's plan.

The operating plan cannot be the controller's plan, or at least it must not be thought of in that light. Therefore, the controller must establish it "through authorized management" and he must coordinate and maintain it the same way. Further, he must see clearly that he himself is not that authorized management. Many a controller has stumbled on this cardinal principle. It is here that he must call on his utmost inner reserves of service motivation—that he may subordinate the urge to give orders and perform a patient, selfless office through the leadership of top and operating management.

This does not mean that the controller can be a weak individual. He will constantly need to sell, to explain, to teach, to urge those representatives of management at all levels who are authorized to exercise line authority that the planning principle may be implemented and a well-planned organization emerge. He must of course, begin with the president or chief executive officer of his company, for all systematic planning, and therefore scientific controllership, begins at the top.

I should like to call particular attention to one other innovation before leaving this part of the definition. The techniques of planning are deliberately subordinated to the idea of the plan itself. The budgeting activity, the sales forecasting, cost standards—all of those control media which accountants, engineers and others have developed to such fine precision—become, when elevated to the field of controllership, only the working tools of the trade. The product to be fashioned with those tools is "an integrated plan for the control of operations."

MEASUREMENT AND INTERPRETATION

The second major function is packed with power which, like all power, must be exerted with utter fidelity to principle. The power of reporting and interpretation is the power to guide, to clarify and to strengthen the men who make the decisions. It is not the power of decision-making. It is the power to keep the ship off the reefs, but not to propel it—to navigate but not to take command.

It will be noted that this function assumes the presence of an effective operating plan, with budgets, procedures and so on, all set up under point number one. The measurement here contemplated is essentially "against approved operating plans and standards." But even where no standards exist, it is the duty of controllership to report and interpret operating results. For this purpose we must of course have accounting and cost systems and accumulate numerous statistical data.

Point two might here again be examined in the light of these explanatory comments:

> 2. To measure performance against approved operating plans and standards, and to report and interpret the results of operations to all levels of management. This function includes the design, installation and maintenance of accounting and cost systems and records, the determination of accounting policy and the compilation of statistical records as required.

Here falls the heavy reporting requirement. Much has been said and written concerning reports to management by very competent practitioners of controllership. Suffice it here to place the subject in focus in the controllership orbit. The form of such reporting is inconsequential to the present subject. Conceivably, the controller might keep management (of which he is a part) adequately informed by verbal reporting only, from a few worksheets and notes, although experience has shown that this would not be the most effective method. The important thing to remember is that the liaison of controllership and decision-making management cannot properly be maintained by sole reliance on a set of periodic statements, no matter how well designed they may be. The statements, and even the written comments thereon, are merely means for contributing to the discharge of a responsibility. The duty is not discharged until management actually understands the facts.

The responsibility for interpretation augments this function and at the same time clarifies it. Interpretation! What an invitation to make an important contribution to a company's welfare! When I am asked simply to provide figures, I am restricted, but there is no limit to my freedom when I am asked to interpret them. But, at the same time, I am conscious of the persistent inner prompting, that my interpretation must be governed by absolute accuracy. Truth demands a sharpening of faculties to analyze and examine, to sift and search again before interpretive conclusions are presented to management. We might almost say that it is the function of controllership always to be right!

Notice again the subordination of techniques to the fundamental purpose. The design of cost systems, the preparation of statements, the long discussions of depreciation rates, inventory policy, valuation and periodic determination of profit generally, all belong (omitting tax considerations) in the category of tools for a more fundamental objective of controllership—namely, the measurement of performance against approved operating plans and standards, and the reporting on an interpretation of the results of operations.

What happens when the measurement of performance has been made, reported and even interpreted? What action is taken and who takes it? The most typical case perhaps is the excess of actual expenditures over budget for a division of the business reporting to the president. Once this situation has been measured, analyzed, reported, interpreted, what is the controller's next move? First, if he is a sound controller, he will have given the same set of facts to both division head and president. It is then the job of the president, not the controller, to take whatever steps are indicated. Neither good organization practice nor acceptable controllership would impose on the controller the responsibility of approving or censuring the action of the division head in exceeding his budget, or even of suggesting a higher budget. This area is for the president and his subordinate to settle between them. The maximum that can be said concerning the controller's influence in the matter is that the clarity of his analysis and his insistence that the facts be understood may impel the proper action.

Similar policy will govern the controller's attitude toward all phases of the operating plan. He has established it through authorized management. In other words, they have set their own budgets and forecasts, he has composed of their planning a forecast of operations, and he is now engaged in measuring performance against the plan. His *modus operandi* is "management by exception." The point where performance fails to conform to the approved plan attracts his scrutiny and the pertinent facts are reported at once to all levels of management concerned. Thus corrections can be made, either in future performance or in the plan itself if that is faulty or impossible of fulfillment. Controllership has done its job. Responsible management has its controls. Now it must use them.

VALIDITY AND EFFECTIVENESS

If, after studying the first two items in the stated function of controllership brought forth by the Institute, there is any doubt about the controller's right and duty to think and talk about any phase whatever of the operations of his company, such a doubt should be utterly dispelled by point three. Within its expansive realm the lid is removed and the controller's imaginative and creative powers are released. Let me repeat this point:

3. To measure and report on the validity of the objectives of the business and on the effectiveness of its policies, organization structure and procedures in attaining those objectives. This includes consulting with all segments of management responsible for policy or action concerning any phase of the operation of the business as it relates to the performance of this function.

Perhaps this is the hardest plank in the platform for most controllers to accept. At the very least, it demands that they raise their eyes from their books, budgets and the other paraphernalia of their trade and look out to the horizons of business. No one could even begin this assignment unless he were a student not only of his own business but of other businesses and indeed of all business. He may even have to leave off analyzing and spend a little time dreaming.

Is this requirement impractical and ethereal? A little reflection I think will make it clear that it is not. Up to this time we have considered the controller in the light of a measure, reporter and interpreter of performance against approved operating plans and standards. What about those phases of business in which standards have not yet been or cannot be established? Is controllership to remain mute in such circumstances?

Or, to carry the matter a step further, who is to raise such questions as should be raised as to the validity of the standards themselves? It would seem that controllership must make absolute judgments as well as those which are only relative to a standard established by another part of management.

Every company has a large mass of objectives—and broadly speaking, it is part of the controller's job to reduce these objectives to manageable fractions. This he does, as already suggested, by means of coordinated planning through authorized management. The import of the point we are discussing is that it is also his province to question the validity of that

9

planning if in his judgment it deserves questioning; and he is entitled to the ear of top management in doing so.

It should now be clear that this prerogative is indispensable to the independence and range of thought and action which the controller must possess. It is only a short step further to say that the validity of the grand objectives of the business—its product planning, market development and research for instance—must also fall within his purview, for the full expression of the idea demands complete subject matter.

As to the effectiveness of policies, organization structure and procedures for the attainment of objectives, controllership must ultimately firmly insist on the right to appraise. How many times has the controller—or one of his lieutenants such as a budget master—assiduously tracked down a failure to perform to standard only to find a faulty policy at the root of the trouble? How many times, in establishing the procedures needed for sound budget administration, has he been confronted with a confused and hazy bit of organization structure, which had to be righted in order to give meaning to the budget?

The times are countless—yet the controller cannot indulge the luxury of frustration at this point. He must deftly, gently criticize and repair, enlisting direct line executive help at whatever level it may be needed. He must, in fact, gradually create universal recognition of the idea that "any phase of the operation of the business" is his business; and he must do it with the minimum of offense.

The summation of point number three, then is contained in a few words typical of the whole case—that on no matter what level of controllership we happen to be working, we must go further than to say that performance failed to meet the standard. We must also ask whether the standard itself makes sense, and we must pursue that question through all the intricacies of the organization until the answer is clear to all concerned.

GOVERNMENT REPORTING AND TAXES

In terms of immediate profit, the controller's responsibilities in the area of government reporting and taxes rightfully demand a high priority on his time and energies. It is precisely for this reason—that the yield from this kind of effort is so immediate and tangible—that this function frequently tends to occupy the spotlight to the exclusion of those more fundamentally significant activities which have already been described. The urgency of decisions in the field of taxes emphasizes this tendency and the net result is that too often the controller finds himself almost completely absorbed in these problems, to the neglect of the area of planning and control which are so vital to the contribution he makes to his company.

Nor can the controller easily delegate this task. There are too many major company policies laden with tax implications. The amortization of emergency facilities is a current example. The effect of dividend policy on the excess profit credit is another. Every controller is familiar with the persistent problem of considering the tax rate for the forthcoming year in order that management may decide intelligently whether an expenditure could more profitably be made this year or next. The examples could be multiplied indefinitely, but these will suffice to illustrate the rather comprehensive understanding of tax law and Internal Revenue Bureau practice which the controller must have in order to administer his company's tax policy.

The Institute's statement of point four in the list of functions is so simple as almost to conceal the breadth of its scope:

> 4. To report to government agencies, as required, and to supervise all matters relating to taxes.

The reporting to government agencies "as required" implies a broad but not exclusive delegation of duty. In the complex business life we are living, in which nearly every phase of a company's activities touches the exercise of governmental authority at some point, certain executives other than the controller may be required to do some reporting. In such cases, the most satisfactory solution would seem to be a system of referral of such reports to the controller's staff for review in advance of filing, for the purpose of insuring consistency and coordination in all of the information concerning the business which moves out and into the hands of government or civic agencies. Required reporting of employment, wage rates, and so on might fall in this category.

It is almost self-evident that the closer the subject matter to be reported comes to the general category of financial and accounting data, the more clear it must be that it falls to the controller and his staff to perform the task.

Reports to the Securities and Exchange Commission, the Department of Commerce and the Treasury Department are the traditional responsibility of the controller, and rightfully so. This leads directly into the field of taxation, in which the controller, by training and long-established practice, is recognized as the officer best qualified to do the job. In doing so, of course, he will rely heavily on experienced tax technicians, either on his own staff or in the public accounting field.

The Institute's specification that the controller is "to supervise all matters relating to taxes" is somewhat vague; I think deliberately so. It was quite evidently intended to be large enough to embrace an area of tax activity performed by most controllers which could well be excluded from a strict definition of controllership. I refer to the negotiation of tax settlements.

Many controllers conclude such settlements with the Commissioner of Internal Revenue, after carrying on all of the required negotiations, and I think we must accept the fact that such an arrangement may be the most practical one, and that it usually brings into operation in behalf of the company the personnel best qualified for the task. At the same time, we must recognize that this duty is not entirely consistent with the rather highly refined staff status of controllership. From the standpoint of pure controllership, other executives should negotiate a tax settlement under the same set of principles that governs the negotiation of the purchase of raw materials, the rental of plant facilities or a union contract.

General practice, however, has pretty well set the scene. In the majority of places, it is understood that the controller will assume the tax negotiating job, and indeed no one else seems to have the slightest disposition to undertake it. This generalization does not hold good everywhere and especially in the larger companies there has been a tendency to place the burden of tax negotiation in the hands of some other financial officer.

When the controller performs this office, he is faced with establishing a procedure and an understanding with his top management under which he has clear conception of the extent of his authority in agreeing to negotiated settlements, and of the boundaries beyond which he must get specific approvals. If he is wise, he will lean rather heavily on the side of enlisting the concurrence of the chief executive officer of his company in tax settlements which he negotiates. Only in this way can he hope to avoid a certain corrosion of that objectivity and detachment with which he views the operations of his company and which is his stock in trade in the practice of controllership. He must remember that every assumption of direct power vitiates correspondingly the vast indirect potential that goes with his staff status.

It will be obvious that the foregoing comments apply with equal validity to certain areas of what might be called financial negotiation other than taxes. Renegotiation is a case in point, as well as defense contract termination settlements. Many controllers have been drawn into the conduct of such negotiations and into a considerable measure of responsibility for settlements as well. This development, of course, is a logical outgrowth of his complete familiarity with the figures involved, but he should protect himself with an adequate understanding as to his limit of authority and in addition will find it profitable, both to the discharge of his office and to the settlement he is negotiating, to include operating management in the negotiating team whenever possible. Above all, he should keep his president informed of his actions and insist on having his decisions ratified.

I have alluded in the first paragraph under this point to the heart of the controllership service in the tax field—the immense value that can come from preventive tax planning. It is the task of controllership not only to scrutinize every contemplated move from the tax standpoint, but sometimes even to initiate thinking concerning possible operating decisions which may have tax benefits.

The importance of this activity cannot be exaggerated. The controller must, by consistent process of education, create an atmosphere of tax consciousness in his organization and inculcate the broad outlines of tax philosophy among his associates. It must become a matter of instinct for the operating heads of his business to refer to him in advance of decision the essential facts concerning proposed moves and transactions. Naturally, he should be in a position to have knowledge concerning the company's planning at a very early stage in its development for the purposes of his own planning and coordinating assignment, but the tax aspect requires special cultivation.

This important area is explored in considerable detail in a recent study issued by Controllership Foundation, "Management Planning for Corporate Taxes." The emphasis of the study is not placed on ways of saving taxes—a subject which is covered in far more detail by the various tax services—but rather on the needs of the organization for recognizing tax situations in ordinary operations before it is too late, and in consciously organizing to consider them. The controller is the key figure in this process.

EXTERNAL INFLUENCES

The fiery test of controllership is its capacity to interpret economic, social and governmental influences and to harness this know-how to the service of the individual company. It is probable that relatively few controllers accept the full responsibility laid down in point number five. It is only fair to say that in very few organizations is the controller charged with the duty of performing this service. Let us re-examine the statement of this responsibility as set forth by the Institute:

> 5. To interpret and report on the effect of external influences on the attainment of the objectives of the business. This function includes the continuous appraisal of economic and social forces and of governmental influences as they affect the operations of the business.

In case this area of activity should appear to any one to be without the scope of controllership, let me inquire if he has been faced in recent years with the task of deciding whether or not his company could profitably adopt the LIFO basis of inventory valuation. After he has made his extensive study of the technical aspects of the problem, including the tax benefits to be derived from the application of LIFO to various segments of inventory—under certain sets of assumptions as to price trends of course—what then? He has had to face the inexorable decision as to whether commodity prices and labor rates in his business can be expected to rise or fall, or do each consecutively, and to what extent. No LIFO decision can be made without facing this issue squarely, and the issue cannot be faced without an intelligent appreciation of the economics of the country and the industry.

Perhaps this example will make it clear that controllership cannot bury itself in the sand with respect to economics. In a much broader sense, however, careful examination of his other responsibilities makes it evident that he cannot discharge them effectively without continuously appraising them to the best of his ability and reporting them regularly within his management.

13

The very act of agreeing upon a forecast of sales volume implies some knowledge of the economic future. An informed reporting on performance against such a forecast requires it. Certainly any adventure into the validity of the objectives of the business would be ill-conceived without basic equipment in the field of applied economics. Nor can the controller ignore the basic social and governmental evolutions taking place before his eyes. Whether he likes them or not, he must be aware that they are affecting his business, and he must appraise the extent of their influence.

This is not to suggest that the controller should be the sole functionary in the field of economics. Other members of the executive group—notably the president and the sales or other executive responsible for forecasting—must exercise the same kind of intelligence. The point made here is that, regardless of the work in this line done by other elements of the business, controllership must, in order to do a complete job, accept the assignment of interpreting and reporting on the effect of external influences on the attainment of the objectives of the business. It must not restrict its opportunities by failing to look outside as well as inside the immediate business operation for answers to the fundamental questions of business management.

There is some evidence of increasing awareness of these facts on the part of controllers. Some of them have, under the prod of unsolved problems, broadened their reading and listening into those fields which have made them more sensitive to the changing currents in the economic and social picture. Some companies, under the stimulus of controllership, have turned their thinking outward through connections with consulting economists. Others have added economists to their staffs, and in a number of instances these men have been assigned to the direction of the controller in order to insure objective presentation of the economic picture for all of management.

This need, for guidance in a complicated field, for controllers already overburdened, must be solved in the manner most suitable to the individual business. The acceptance of the responsibility outlined in point number five is today's leading challenge to the initiative and resources of controllership.

PROTECTION FOR THE ASSETS

Here we return to charted waters. Practically all controllers and most of their assistants enjoy an unimpeachable mastery of the Institute's point six, which reads as follows:

> 6. To provide protection for the assets of the business. This function includes establishing and maintaining adequate internal control and auditing, and assuring proper insurance coverage.

The elements of this responsibility which are of particular interest in the current stage of development of controllership are those in which the specified responsibility is functionally discharged. The provision of proper insurance coverage is an example. It is not vital that the direct responsibility for determining an amount of insurance coverage required and for purchasing that coverage be lodged in the controller's office. It is essential, however, that, regardless of who buys the insurance, the controller be given the latitude required to make an independent judgment as to the insurance needs of the company. By proper organization arrangement, he must, at the very least, report his findings on this subject to the president. If he feels that the insurance coverage is inadequate, it is his duty to insist that the defect be remedied, the only acceptable alternative being an explicit overruling of his recommendation.

To a lesser degree, the same comments apply to the maintenance of adequate internal control. Much of the procedure required for proper internal control may be found within the controller's own organization, but his specifications on this point must be respected wherever assets of the company exist. For example, a branch plant cost accounting department might well report direct to the plant manager, but internal control procedures therein (as well as procedures of cost determination, etc.) should be the functional responsibility of the controller, and he must be equipped with organization arrangements which will permit him to exercise such authority.

Internal auditing is properly an extension of the techniques of internal control. It belongs unquestionably in the sphere of controllership activity. In some companies, for reasons peculiar thereto, the auditing function has been set up to report to the president or even to the Board of Directors. Assuming the presence of responsible controllership, and an annual audit by an independent firm of public accountants, such an arrangement is neither necessary nor desirable.

The broad responsibility of providing protection for the assets of the business demands the careful attention of the controller, as well as a fair share of his administrative time. It is a duty which cannot be neglected, but must not be permitted to endanger the performance of those infinitely more vital services described in the other points in the Institute's concept of controllership. The fairly liberal use of the services of insurance consultants and public accountants will frequently make it possible to carry on these activities effectively with a minimum of time invested.

ORGANIZATION STATUS

The cultivation of controllership requires a favorable climate—else it will not bear fruit. The status of the controller within his organization—regardless of his title—must be such that the principle he embodies may be given full expression.

This matter has been discussed and debated at great length. In recent years it has become evident that a statement of the proper organization status of the controller was badly needed. Controllers Institute of America undertook the task of constructing such a statement, by referring the problem to the committee, mentioned earlier in this paper, which prepared the Institute's concept of the controllership function. The statement of the organization status of the controller which that committee evolved, and which was subsequently accepted by the Board of Directors is as follows:

1. The controller should be an executive officer at the policy-making level responsible directly to the chief executive officer of the business. His appointment or removal should require the approval of the Board of Directors.
2. The controller should be required by the Board of Directors to present directly periodic reports covering the operating results and financial condition of the business, together with such other information as it may request.
3. The controller should preferably be a member of the Board of Directors, and all other top policy-making groups. At a minimum he should be invited to attend all meetings of such groups with the right to be heard.

It will have become evident by this time that, just as not all controllers are discharging fully the proper functions of controllership, so not all controllers are placed in the ideal relationship to the chief executive officers and Boards of Directors of their companies. It is natural that this should be so, considering the relative newness of the modern concept of controllership which we are discussing. The important thing, in any given situation, is not so much whether the ideal has been reached as whether the perfect concept is gaining acceptance from year to year in the minds of the controller, his associates, his staff, his top management, his Board. There is no one in this field who cannot gain from a study of and an adherence to the principles involved, for by this course these ideas gradually but surely find expression in the affairs of the business.

It should also be clear that the exercise of the controllership functions and the achievement of proper organization status do not usurp the slightest prerogative of operating management or of the president. If the controller does his job skillfully, he will never hear such an accusation. He is properly a member of the president's staff. He may carry the title of vice president, but should not be considered an assistant to the president in the sense in which that designation is usually intended. He must be particularly aware of the need to avoid the impression of actually making the decisions for which others are responsible, though he can and should consciously influence those decisions by the impartial presentation of fact.

EXHIBIT 1

WHAT IS CONTROLLERSHIP?

The concept of the function of controllership, as developed by Controllers Institute's Committee on Ethics and Eligibility Standards, and approved by the National Board of Directors on September 25, 1949, follows:

1. To establish, coordinate and maintain, through authorized management, an integrated plan for the control of operations. Such a plan would provide, to the extent required in the business, cost standards, expense budgets, sales forecasts, profit planning, and programs for capital investment and financing, together with the necessary procedures to effectuate the plan.
2. To measure performance against approved operating plans and standards, and to report and interpret the results of operations to all levels of management. This function includes the design, installation and maintenance of accounting and cost systems and records, the determination of accounting policy and the compilation of statistical records as required.
3. To measure and report on the validity of the objectives of the business and on the effectiveness of its policies, organization structure and procedures in attaining those objectives. This includes consulting with all segments of management responsible for policy or action concerning any phase of the operation of the business as it relates to the performance of this function.
4. To report to government agencies, as required, and to supervise all matters relating to taxes.
5. To interpret and report on the effect of external influences on the attainment of the objectives of the business. This function includes the continuous appraisal of economic and social forces and of governmental influences as they affect the operations of the business.
6. To provide protection for the assets of the business. This function includes establishing and maintaining adequate internal control and auditing, and assuring proper insurance coverage.

EXHIBIT 2

THAT WORD "CONTROL"[1]

There seems to be a tendency for controllers to avert their eyes and assume a look of injured innocence when they are referred to as having or exerting "control." Perhaps this reluctance to be identified with "control" is a contributing cause to the persistence in modern business of the old-fashioned title "comptroller," an etymologically incorrect word derived from the French and traceable to the antiquities of bookkeeping.

Now many words in the English language are commonly endowed with various shadings of meaning, and we move easily from one to another in our conversation. The word "control," when applied to the controller of a business enterprise, has a specialized meaning, which is not clearly understood, even by the top strata of management, much less the financial public and press.

Perhaps we can throw light on this shading of meaning by mentioning a few things that the word "control" in this usage does not include. "Control," as here used, does not signify the kind of control over a business which a majority shareholder enjoys. It does not refer to any part of the control centered in the Board of Directors or the president. It does not include line authority for making or carrying out policy or operating decisions, except in the particular sphere of financial operations heretofore described, and even there the authority is carefully circumscribed to the extent that there is a functioning treasurer in the organization.

What then is left for our definition? Perhaps it will be useful to say that the type of control exercised by controllership is the presence in a business of that force which guides it to a predetermined objective by means of predetermined policies. It does not steer the course, but it informs operating management of any significant deviation from it. It never issues orders, but it sees and knows all, and makes plain to the man in charge what he must do to achieve the prescribed aim.

Viewed in this light, no controller need shrink from his title, nor hesitate to exercise the control that it implies. "Budgetary control," an accepted term, is a starting point, and once the controller has mastered the techniques of supervising a budget system without encroaching on anyone's decision-making prerogatives, he will have absorbed most of the philosophy of control. He will be skilled in the science of providing effective controls for his business and making them work.

---

[1]*Editors' Note: This item accompanied the article although not specifically referred to. It is presented here because it sheds light on discussions of control as presented by Mr. Peirce.*

CONTROLLERSHIP MOTIVATION †

by

James L. Peirce

IN recent years the controller's range of thought has been appreciably broadened. Perhaps the time has come when it should also be deepened. In this process, we soon encounter the bed rock of motivation and blast it out for examination.

Sometimes the individual who allows himself to think below the surface on this subject is disappointed at what he finds. His own motives may be confused and even misdirected. We have gone far enough in the development of the controllership science to know what our functions should be. Are we prepared to uncover the motives which activate and stimulate those functions? It is my conviction that we are.

Controllership, under whatever corporate title it may be practiced, has entered the abode of top management as a permanent resident. The planning and control principle, with budgeting, forecasting and accounting as primary tools, is at last being embraced in the management philosophy of a great segment of North American business.

For the past six years, a thoughtful statement of the functions of controllership has been publicized by Controllers Institute of America. It is fair to say that this statement has not been seriously challenged. It would not be fair, however, to say that all the facets of the definition have been tested sufficiently to prove them.

It is one thing to maintain a plan for the control of operations, for example, but quite another to report on the validity of the objectives of the business. It is well understood why and how the controller is to interpret the results of operations to all levels of management, but it is not as well understood that he cannot function completely without continuously appraising the economic and social forces which are affecting his company.

It is reasonable to suppose that these areas, where apparently thus far relatively few controllers have trod, will be fully developed in time. Meanwhile there are large numbers of controllers who seem to be still in the earlier stages—occupying themselves almost exclusively with accounting matters—and here the growing body of controllership inquiry must lend its help. We must accelerate the adoption of the newer concepts. We must

---

†Presented at the 1955 Eastern and Midwestern Conferences, Controllers Institute of America (CIA). Reprinted from *The Controller*, August 1955, pp. 367-369, 396-399, copyright 1955, with permission of the Financial Executives Institute, 10 Madison Avenue, P.O. Box 1938, Morristown, NJ 07962-1938. (201) 898-4600.

knock on the mental doors of both controllers and presidents until these ideas are admitted. The demand for seasoned controllership is growing so rapidly that the question now is whether or not its practitioners are up to it. In business everywhere there is evidence to be found of the need for better planning and for the control that must accompany it—and not only the need, but what is even more important, the realization of it. A competitive economy more rugged than business has ever before experienced is posing this challenge.

THE PLATFORM

Fortunately, there is a clearly lighted path to the fulfillment of this opportunity and the elevation of practical controllership to new usefulness. The Institute's statement of controllership functions [*Editors' Note: see Exhibit 1 on page 18*], already alluded to, constitutes an effective platform for action.

In this distillation of years of experience, reams of writing and hours of debate, will be found 244 words of surpassing significance to business management. Most controllers have read it dozens of times; many have undertaken rigid self-analysis in relation to it; and most of those I have talked with confess that they get lost at some point in its seemingly bottomless depths.

This six-point summary occupies an indispensable place in the chain of reasoning on which these reflections are based; however, it is not my intention to dissect this platform, nor to discuss its individual parts. This has already been done and is a matter of record. The functions have been practiced sufficiently to be proven sound. I should like therefore to use this opportunity to probe a little deeper in the effort to learn something about the driving force behind them.

PERSONAL MOTIVATION

It is here that we confront squarely our chosen topic—motivation. It is here also that we must peel off the superficial layer of veneer and examine ourselves as executives and as human beings. For nothing will move without a force to impel it. No idea will become manifest in accomplishment without the motive which animates it.

It can hardly be denied that the primary impulsion of any man is the irresistible urge to express himself. Income is, of course, one of the primary needs, but it has been shown that the enjoyment of the things which income provides is basically an expression of the man's innate urge for self-expression. Even when salary requirements have been satisfied, the individual discovers that he is still dominated by the inner pressure to express himself more and more completely. He is driven to give voice to the indigenous qualities with which he has been endowed by his Creator.

Now I know that each of us has his own philosophy concerning the composition of a man. I will not try to convert you to mine, except to say that I do not subscribe to the cynical theory that all motivation is selfish. To express one's true self is exactly the opposite of being selfish, and I think this conclusion is nowhere better illustrated than among controllers.

For controllership thrives on a diet of service motivation. The most successful controller is the one who has so disciplined his thinking that he is in harmony with the objectives of a great service to business. He is required to devote himself to equipping his fellow executives with information and with the tools of control. He must support them with sound judgment and impartial advice. He must contribute freely to their decisions to the limit of his ability, with full knowledge that he can neither make those decisions himself nor claim credit for them–and he must never count the cost.

Now this service motivation is not peculiar to controllership. It is also a characteristic of other staff functions—personnel relations for instance—but controllership is as pure an example as can be found. It does not approach maximum stature when adulterated with operating duties, either conferred or usurped, and it must curb ambition in this direction if it aspires to ideal performance.

This becomes evident as we observe, in the first of the controller's official duties that he is to arrange and coordinate one of the most complex techniques of modern management—the plan for the control of operations—without any direct enforcing authority whatever. To him is given only the right to sell his wares, and he must thereupon engineer this mechanism entirely "through authorized management." This assignment requires adherence to the rule of seeking his own progress in the progress of others, however altruistic this may sound.

THE HONEST PURPOSE

Moreover, we cannot escape the need for old-fashioned honesty of purpose in discharging these duties. The obligation to measure performance requires it, and the charge to interpret the results of operations does also. Even the specification that all levels of management be informed demands integrity of a high order in the controller's dealings with his associates. More so does the reporting on the effectiveness of policies, organization structure and procedures in attaining the objectives of the business.

The controllers I have known take their responsibilities very seriously indeed. The desire to be fair in their judgments, and the pitfalls of hasty or biased appraisals are a constant concern to most of them. It is easy to provide figures taken from a set of books, but it is quite another matter to see that those figures do not give rise to incorrect inferences on the part of those who use them.

We can only begin to imagine the havoc which a controller without scruple might cause. I am not here referring to cheating the government in tax practice or his company in expense accounts—although these deviations are bad enough in themselves—but rather to the far more subtle temptation to place shadings of meaning on the facts which further those aims which are to his liking. The authority to interpret is a heavy responsibility, and the controller must be dedicated to the uncovering and communication of impersonal truth. He can never lean toward either side of an issue because of the personalities involved.

Nor is this "bearing false witness" confined to deliberate distortion of the facts. It is all too easy to erect a mental barrier against the inspirations of the sales department, for example, because they do not conform to our conservative pattern of thinking. It is true that controllers devote much effort to deflating ill-conceived proposals with hard facts—yet they must not indulge a negative attitude on a "guilty until proved innocent" premise. It is not consistent with the honest purpose that we should delight in proving our creative associates wrong.

PROFITS AND COMMUNITY OBJECTIVES

Company philosophy must also be considered, however. To a large extent the controller's motivation is identified with that of the business of which he is a part. In times not too long past, this motive was profit, almost exclusively. Today we have advanced to the conviction that happy employees are as essential as happy stockholders, and the base has been widened to include customers, the community and government, the last especially where national defense is concerned. Business literature in recent years has established the case for warmer and more social objectives for the once chilly corporate being. This metamorphosis has direct meaning for the controller. He, no less than the president of his company, must be attuned to the new atmosphere. If he is not, his interpretations and comments will be flavored with attitudes outmoded.

Upon the controller is conferred a unique privilege in the Institute's definition. He is asked to measure and report on the validity of the objectives of the business. To absorb the impact of this language takes a lot of thinking, and to make it one's own requires even more.

One of the easier ways to avoid the mental labor required to understand this provision is to pass it by quickly on the assumption that it is the duty of the president and board of directors. Doubtless it is—but the framers of the concept had a clear conviction that it was the duty of the controller also.

Note that it is not his duty to *establish* the objectives of the business—only to measure and report on their validity. Perhaps even this much is beyond the range of some of us at present. Even so, it is not too early to begin thinking about it.

As a starting point, we might ask ourselves a few pertinent questions: *Does our operation have a profit objective, and is it a valid one? Does it have stated objectives for product improvement? What is its management thinking concerning expansion of markets? What is its philosophy on employee relations and executive development?*

Now I do not propose that the controller begin making a project of each of these questions, and I think he should be particularly cautious about advancing unwanted suggestions in fields in which he is not qualified. Nevertheless he should be thinking deeply in all these areas. His very exploration and discussion of them with his associates will qualify him to perform better his essential job of coordinating the company's planning. For all these fundamental questions of motivation of the business underlie its planning.

Little by little, evaluation of objectives leads to better planning. Better planning leads to better control. The controller may choose to *measure* a long time before he decides to *report* on the validity of objectives. Having gone through this thought process he will find himself so closely identified with the motivation of his business that he can no longer be accused of being lost in books and figures. He will have been revitalized with ideas, and his contribution to his company's progress will be augmented correspondingly.

But for many controllers, the first battle is with the spectre of doubt that he reads in the glances of his associates—the entrenched fallacy that these things are none of his business. This enemy will fade away with the dawn of the conviction that everything that concerns the company is the controller's business. The governing viewpoint must be correct, however. His treatment of top policy objectives must be in the dispassionate, impersonal light that bespeaks a mind rightly motivated.

THE PROFIT MOTIVE

I should not like to leave the impression of having discarded the time-tested profit motive, with which controllers have been so intimately connected. The need for an adequate profit is inherent in our competitive system, and is the force which may be credited with much of its initiative. I do, however, wish to emphasize the need for an *enlightened* profit motive.

One of the definitions for "profit" in Webster's dictionary is "valuable results; useful consequences." In this sense, the profit motive is bathed in the light of purity, because we can evaluate our results or consequences as broadly as we wish.

The question of immediate profit, for example, may sometimes be sublimated to the needs of public goodwill. The well-adjusted controller knows the meaning of public relations, stockholder relations, employee relations, and customer relations. These are such vital considerations that he cannot afford to be ignorant concerning them. If he is to be guided by an enlightened profit motive, he must be able to visualize, in each management decision, the "valuable results; useful consequences," whether or not these are manifested in the dollars which compose the immediate transaction.

Even in the narrower sense, however, the comfortable old-fashioned profit motive—we will assume it has been enlightened—is still valid as a guide to business. A company consistently returning a fair profit is *usually* pretty well adjusted to the more spiritual demands of the day. It usually ranks high in the calibre and balance of its management personnel, and, by the same token seldom is found ignoring public and community values.

Furthermore, a cost reduction effort usually contributes to profit, as does an improvement in procedures or planning. The addition of new sales volume (with an acceptable profit margin) works in the same direction. None of the minor or major moves taken by a company with the profit objective in view are harmful to it if long-range wisdom is exercised. Therefore the criterion of the controller—*Does the proposed action influence profit favorably?*—is generally valid.

It is in this sense that the words "profit planning" were used in the first of the six controllership functions. It obviously is of no value to plan income and costs unless a reasonable profit remains; and this profit must perhaps be planned first.

Many companies have, during recent years, begun to realize, sometimes with sorrow, the importance of maintaining a profit. In the inflationary years which we have come through, new financing could never have provided the mountain of new capital that industry has needed. In the long run, it is the function of profits in excess of dividend requirements to keep the business alive—for no business can live long without growing.

This being true, we must admit that profit is the *visible* motive at least for manufacturing an article and selling it—that, tempered with the vision of service to customer, employee and country, it is a reliable enough motive for doing business, and that controllership must therefore accord it appropriate respect.

PLANNING AND CONTROL MOTIVATION

Specifically, however, there is a driving force behind the planning and control idea. Perhaps we can define it by examining the complex structure of business and its manifold needs.

It is certain that the most clearly defined unit in the economic scene is the individual company or business. There was a time, of course, when these units were generally small and easily manageable by one man. As they grew they took on the delicate intricacies of organization. First, departmentalization began—then came branches, and re-groupings known as divisions–and now we have the refinements of decentralized industry.

Strictly speaking, this development has never been without planning. It could not have taken place without planning. Only recently, however, has there been a coordinated effort to plan all the affairs of a business, in integrated fashion, and to control action to the plan.

It is difficult to say exactly what brought this into being. In retrospect, the gap has always been waiting to be filled. There can be no sustained profits, no fulfillment of growth and service objectives, without careful planning and conscientious control. Perhaps this realization sprang from the chaos of organization without direction. Whatever its source, the incentive to plan and control is alive and growing.

The techniques of this idea have now become simple enough. First comes planning for a future period—comprehensive and detailed, and translated by the controllership skill into the language of figures. Then, when the period is under way, reporting takes place—by the exception method and with corollary interpretation. The indicated action becomes the third step—and this action may be either to bring operations into harmony with the plan or to revise the plan. This simple three-part formula, planning-reporting-action, is the *modus operandi* of the planning and control principle.

As this idea developed, it was accompanied by the demand for a man in the organization who could make it work. This task is becoming known as controllership, and it is being entrusted more and more to an individual known as the controller, though frequently to an officer with another title having the controllership duties.

The impact of this change on the controller of two decades ago is marked. Then he was usually known as the man in charge of accounting, cost analysis, taxes and auditing. These responsibilities persist in the statement of functions [referenced] earlier in this paper.

Accounting, however, has been sublimated to the broader task of measuring performance and interpreting the results of operations. His beloved cost work has become not an end but only the means for maintaining a plan for the control of operations, and for reporting in detail thereon, in order that the control might be effective. The old functions are engulfed in new and broader ones which insist that he appraise critically both the objectives of the business and the effect of economic forces on their attainment. Of the former functions, only tax administration and internal auditing have retained their separate identity.

Basically the seed of controllership is found in business itself—in its modern form of organization and in the necessity of guiding this young giant. We have modern controllership not because the controllers wished it, even though their insight has brought it about. The actual motivation is found in the discernment on the part of management that a means of planning a forward course and of controlling the business to that course is indispensable to the further progress of industry. This demand cannot be denied nor ignored.

WHAT CONTROLLERS MUST DO

In order that controllership may answer this call, it seems to me that controllers individually must adopt a decisive program. They must forsake the defensive and take the offensive in this battle for scientific management.

Perhaps the first step is the effort to think as management rather than as accounting. This requires some delicate mental distinctions. I am told that one of the stubborn problems in the movement to make foremen a part of management is to get them to think as management. They persist in thinking as workers endowed with supervisory duties. This dilemma may contain a hint for us.

Every controller might take a few quiet moments to ask himself the question, *Do I really think as management or do I think only as a hired accountant?* It is a searching question, which leads to other questions:

Do I approach the vital problems which my business is facing with the viewpoint of those responsible for solving them; or do I mentally draw away and retire into the secure realm of the figure producer, content to let others grapple with the decisions?

Do I think of myself as management assigned to the controllership function, or only as a controller aspiring to become management?

The answers are all-important, for "as he thinketh in his heart, so is he." It is a profitable exercise for a controller to declare to himself "I am a part of management" and then to ask himself if he really believes what he is saying. An honest look in his mental mirror may tell him that he does not. There are too many references in current business literature to controllers preparing "reports for management," in such a manner as to leave the implication that management is something apart from them, to which they merely report.

This donning the mantle of management involves doffing the robes of the professional accountant. Although industrial accounting is a major responsibility of the controller, it is entirely subordinate to the task of operating a business properly by means of planning and control principles. Therefore he must leave the finesse of the profession to the public accountants, rely on them for guidance in taxes and the determination of periodic net income, and practice controllership.

He must also separate his assignment from finance, even though frequently he will be called upon to do both. The treasurer's function is akin to the responsibility for an operating department, except that it deals with money rather than materials and manpower. The pure function of controllership does not operate; it supports the operations of others.

COMPENSATION AND PROMOTION

This leads to another phase of motivation which is much thought of but little discussed—the question of the compensation of controllers and their channels for promotion.

So far as the former is concerned, it should be measured by the contribution which the controller makes to his company. Controllers are prone to resent the fact that they are out-compensated by sales managers—yet the latter must produce or go, and their relatively high business mortality attests this understanding. When controllers have made their service as valuable in the minds of top management as that of the business-getting function—that is, when they have produced a high-calibre planning and control coordination and have convinced all concerned of its value, they will no longer trail at the end of the management parade.

Then we will no longer read announcements of controllers being "promoted" to the position of treasurer. If the controllership job is well done and adequately recognized, such a move is not a promotion. Neither will controllers be seeking movement into operating jobs as an outlet for expanding creative talent. Their principal channels of progress will be the presidency or a larger sphere of controllership, and let them consider well the possibilities of the latter course within their own present organizations.

To realize these opportunities, we must see the unlimited contribution to be made by inspired controllership to the progress of all business. We must relinquish the charms of the accounting science and discipline our thinking toward the management science. We must reject operating duties, which would adulterate the high work awaiting us. We must insist on adequate staffs to carry out our assignments, and yet refrain from "empire-building." We must, in short, cultivate straightforward and clear motives for all that we think, say and do.

HOW CAN IT BE SOLD?

One of the questions most frequently asked concerning the application of the controllership idea is, *What can be done to sell it to management?* This is almost a separate subject in itself. Underlying this eternal sales campaign there must be an understanding of the principles of controllership on the part of the controller himself. To put it another way, a controller who is saturated with this philosophy and thoroughly convinced of the need for it in his business will perform a natural sales job that will be relatively effortless. From the motivation of his own convictions he will convince others.

Let us suppose you do not make use of the planning and control principle in your organization—in fact, that you do not even use budgets. Now permit me to recommend that you ask yourself a few questions, linked together to establish a chain of reasoning. And let me further suggest that you give careful thought to each question, and find in the recesses of your thought a considered answer.

First: *Have you ever faced squarely the fact that the reason your top management group does not "buy" the budget idea may be that you yourself are lukewarm about it?*

Have you too quickly assumed that because your business has sharp peaks and valleys, sales forecasting is not for you?

Have you been talked out of a scientific approach to planning because you cannot meet the argument: "We have been making a satisfactory profit without it"?

Have you accepted the subtle suggestion that everyone is too busy to do a job of orderly forward planning?

Have you subconsciously rested on the hazy conclusion that your business is different from all others and therefore not subject to the same management principles?

If your answer has to be in the affirmative, you are not alone. Each of these arguments has taken its toll in the battle for better management.

Let us go a step further:

Are you failing to make the best use of modern planning and control technique because you have a misconception of budgeting?

Are you thinking of it mainly as a pressure device with which to get the most work out of people at the least cost, rather than as a system whereby people can establish their own yardsticks and, in harmony with supervision, improve their own performance?

Do you think of the controller and his staff as police officers charged with enforcing compliance with the budget, instead of placing this responsibility in the line organization where it belongs?

If any of these quite prevalent notions is clinging to your concept of budgeting, there is still ample time to rid yourself of them.

Another step: *Are you thinking of budgeting as simply setting a standard for each expense item rather than as the statement in figures of detailed operating planning?*

Does the budgeting idea loom up in your mind as a new technique, and a rather expensive one at that, to be superimposed on your existing structure of accounting, costs and estimating, rather than as a change to an operation fully coordinated by means of planning and control?

Have you failed to realize that budgeting of expenses is only a segment of a company-wide planning and control structure, which ought to include every item in the profit and loss statement, as well as a financial program which would control every item in the balance sheet?

If the answer is yes, you may have a clue to your inability to sell the controllership idea.

And now let me ask one more trio of impolite questions: *Are you by any chance one of those who insists that the planning and control idea never makes any progress in your organization for lack of top management support?*

Do you give up too soon because you happen to be the controller of a branch or subsidiary and cannot make your distant home office see it the way you do?

Finally, and in summary:

Are you completely sold yourself on the package you are trying to sell others?

The last question of course is the heart of this entire matter of selling controllership. If the controller lives it in his business affairs, he can impart it to those around him. It is my honest conviction that we who ask how to sell this idea will find that it is selling itself once we have mastered it well enough to express it whenever the opportunity occurs in our business day.

OBJECTIVE MANAGEMENT

I hope that the foregoing comments have offered at least one view of the unlimited fields ahead for controllership rightly motivated. There is, of course, a philosophical framework to every kind of work, and perhaps before concluding it would be well to touch on this phase of our chosen field.

There is no section of management which must place so high a premium on pure objectivity as the controller. He must keep himself equally free from sales enthusiasm, engineering exactitude and the power-leadership of the president's office (and this is not to deny that salesmen must sometimes be exact, engineers enthusiastic and presidents humbly receptive). Or turn to other functions—purchasing, industrial relations or research, for instance—and you find that each has its requisite attitude, that each reacts to any new proposal in the way that best suits its assigned aim.

This is natural and doubtless beneficial. It does, however, leave the obvious gap. Only the controller can afford to be completely objective. He alone will not retard his achievement by being objective. In fact, he will further it.

Now a trained business analyst, possessed of all the facts, and devoted to objectivity of thought, is an asset worth having in any business. Add to this the know-how to coordinate an effective planning and control system, and his contribution multiplies. All this presupposes his willingness to delegate to someone else such projects as organizing the accounting department to get earlier monthly closings and arguing with the tax authorities. It also rests on his ability to keep free of operating duties which should be performed by others, and which, if he succumbs to the temptation to acquire them, will hinder fulfillment of the controllership opportunity.

All these considerations find their source in the fibre of thinking that the controller is developing from year to year. The core of this fibre, it seems to me, lies in correct motivation, and for this reason I think the controller should study searchingly his own motives and the reasoning which supports them. Only by this means will he unfold a self-sustained set of convictions and the moral courage to uphold them.

CONTROLLERSHIP AND ACCOUNTING: A CONTRAST [†]

by
James L. Peirce

THE theme underlying all of the ideas to which I shall try to give expression in this paper is that controllership and accounting are two distinct and separate sciences, and must be practiced accordingly. If this hypothesis arouses an instinctive resistance in anyone's thought, may I ask that he reserve judgment until we have time to explore it. If, on the other hand, there is complete accord, and the assertion fails to excite any interest at all, let me beg the reader to examine with me the recesses of his thinking, and find out to what extent either he or I may be wedded to obsolete concepts.

Now the relationship between the sciences of controllership and accounting, if we may call them sciences, is extremely complex. They are tangent at some points and they appear to overlap at others. They are closely entwined in the thinking of management and, of course, the public and press. I believe we have reached the point where they must be disentangled, for the benefit of both and of all business management.

As a first step, let me mention one or two of the important achievements of accounting. Perhaps this will make it easier to show you how heavily controllership must rely upon accounting and that it must acknowledge the leadership of accounting in certain essential fields of thought.

THE SCIENCE OF ACCOUNTING

When I consider the immense debt that business owes the accounting science, the first thing that comes to mind is the concept of periodic net income. This subject, about which tomes have been written, underlies the whole structure of financial conversation. What are the earnings? How do they compare with a year ago? We accept the published figures quite readily, even though, as accountants or controllers, we are far more sophisticated than the financial public concerning the latitude exercised in arriving at those figures.

[†]Presented at a joint meeting of the Hamilton Control of the Controllers Institute of America and the Hamilton and District Chartered Accountants Association, Hamilton, Ontario, April 1953. Reprinted from *The Canadian Chartered Accountant*, July 1953, pp. 5-10, with permission of the Canadian Institute of Chartered Accountants. This article was also published in *The Controller*, September 1953, pp. 410-412, 429-432.

Though we may debate at length the myriad questions surrounding profit determination, we must admit that the profession has done very well. The pendulum of opposing opinions tends to run down, and we find ourselves accepting, pretty much at face value, the certified reports of corporate earnings.

Need I labor this eulogizing with other illustrations? I think not. When you read a certified balance sheet, you have a certain confidence in its valuations. True, you are aware of differing accounting interpretations—yet the accounting science has confined these differences to understandable , dimensions. The most cynical will admit that net worth is a term with meaning, providing the accounts are audited by a reputable firm.

This leads to a characteristic of accounting that is important to the present discussion. Many years ago, accountants made a discovery which is valid today. They found that to dissociate themselves from individual businesses and to establish themselves independently—in much the same manner as the lawyers—afforded them important advantages.

They could, under this arrangement, become immeasurably more objective. They could be free to express their judgments without fear of undue influence by their employers. They could see the problems and internal workings of many companies in many industries and thereby broaden their experience. They could, through formal association, establish professional ethics, and join together in the development of accounting principles. Their employers, later called "clients," naturally relied more heavily upon their findings. This independent *modus operandi* contained all the ingredients of success, and public accounting prospered accordingly.

PROGRESS OF PUBLIC ACCOUNTING

As we move forward in the history of this unique movement, we find public accountants' certificates becoming the keystone of the arch upon which rests the confidence of public and press. We find public accounting working hand in hand with the legal profession—developing the essential financial facts acceptable in our courts. We find accounting principles being expounded and argued in accounting periodicals, in which public accountants play a dominant role owing to the wide range of their experience.

In the field of tax practice, too, public accounting has seized undisputed leadership. Its versatile staffs furnish the essential tax thinking for thousands of corporations, and represent them successfully in relationships with the tax authorities.

Then, more recently, we have become aware of the development of public accounting in newer fields: the installation of cost systems, and counselling industry in the preparation of figures to be used in governmental relationships, as in renegotiation, price redetermination, and contract termination. Because they are qualified by experience, reputation, and integrity, public accountants have been asked to assume heavy burdens of this kind during the past 12 years.

Now I do not intend these remarks to imply any disparagement of the contributions which private accountants, or industrial accountants as we have sometimes called men in private industry, have made to accounting knowledge. Their talks and published articles in the field contradict any such inference. But I shall try to advance the point that because industrial accounting is necessarily subservient to the science called controllership, it can never achieve equivalent status with independent public accounting in guiding the development of the science of accounting and acting as its guardian.

I make mention of the controller's debt to the accounting science because I respect it. I feel that we must accord its practitioners the first place of authority in accounting theory and practice. Controllers must resist the temptation to compete with accountants, in order that they may practice a new and challenging science of their own. If they practice controllership successfully, they will use freely the accumulated wisdom of the devotees of accounting, but will be forced to give their best energies to their own field. This is the parting of the ways and controllership will now demand their full allegiance.

THE SCIENCE OF CONTROLLERSHIP

The reader may well question the use of the word "science" with reference to controllership. Dictionary definitions only give rise to minuscule distinctions and idle conversation, but I think we may assume that if management is a science, as is so well argued by the American Management Association, then controllership is a phase of that science. It is only a small further step to designating it a science in itself. My reason for using the term is that controllership has its foundation in definite principles, can be stated by means of rather precise rules, and is eminently successful if practiced according to those rules.

These principles and rules are perhaps best approached in the framework of an aim and attitude. The aim is to control a business operation so that it may perform up to its maximum capabilities, the word "control" being used in a very special functional sense. The attitude is characterized by a deep service motivation, which delights in mining, refining, and delivering facts about the business which are essential to the making of operating decisions. It is also characterized by a sharpened sense of organization function, under which it refrains from making those decisions or being placed in a position of responsibility for them.

Now, let us examine briefly the contributions which controllership is making to management. The practice of controllership is the exercise by a trained mind of the techniques of control. What are these techniques? What is "control"? [*Editors' Note: see Exhibit 2 on page 19.*]

THE CONTROL PROCESSES

In our own special sense, the word "control" always includes three component processes: the first is the adoption of a plan; the second is reporting of actual performance as compared with the plan; the third is making decisions and taking action. The formula is as simple as that!

To illustrate the principle of control, let us take the manufacturing operation as an example. The plan to be established contains elements familiar to all of you: an expected level of production in sufficient detail, a departmentalized flexible budget for direct labor and factory overhead, and a standard cost system with standard labor times and rates for the operations to be performed. This is the plan for the factory. Using it, we can fit it into the overall plan for the business, compute standard product costs for pricing and inventory purposes, and so on.

The second step in the control process is reporting performance against the plan. This, too, is a familiar task. It is discharged by means of a combination of statements, written comments, and conversation. The purpose is to make the essential facts clear to manufacturing management, including foremen, superintendents, department managers, and the top manufacturing executive. The essential facts consist of a comparison of actual with planned performance, in sufficient detail that every fraction of the operation, and thereby the whole, may be controlled.

The third step is action. When the performance picture is completely clear, the decisions to be made begin to be clear as well. If the reporting is thoughtful rather than perfunctory, creative and forceful rather than confined to conventional forms, the control tool will be sharp. Action will follow. Output and costs will be controlled.

If we have exceeded budget, corrective measures can be initiated. If actual labor time, as shown by daily efficiency reports, is higher than standard, remedial steps may be taken. Note too that if these excesses are attributable to faulty standards or budgets, these must be adjusted accordingly, and this action will alter the plan itself.

The outcome of this activity is a factory doing its work within the ordered discipline of control. We are controlling to predetermined standards. We are applying the technique of management by exception to control its performance.

THE CONTROLLER'S PART IN THE PROCESS

Where does the controller fit into this pattern? First, I think we must recognize that the controller is not one man but a group of men. For our purposes, the controller and his staff are one, and we shall refer to this one as the controller. Actually, the controller must here be thought of as a function, or a force, rather than as an individual. Controllership may be practiced in his behalf, in delimited areas, by a budget manager, a factory accountant, or any other designated individual on the controller's staff.

Let us consider, then, the controller's part in the process of control of the manufacturing operation which we have been using for our example. It seems evident that he cannot himself establish the budgets or standards. Many controllers have tried it and failed, simply because no one takes seriously an operating standard established by the controller alone. Manufacturing management must participate, and top management must lend the weight of its authority. No standard or budget is worth anything if it is not responsibly accepted by the entire line structure of organization, reaching to the top executive level.

Furthermore, the controller cannot initiate the action required in the control process. He cannot himself issue the instructions or change the method of operating. That is the prerogative of the manufacturing management. If he crossed this line, he would be stepping into the shoes of the responsible operating management and would no longer be a controller.

What then does he do? Well, first, before the control process could even be launched, someone had to see the necessity for the proper standards, design the procedures required to provide these standards, and then install the system—all, of course, working hand in hand with operating management. This entire area of thought is the province of the controller.

Then, when the system has been installed, someone will have to measure actual performance against the approved standards, and report and interpret the operating results from period to period. This too is the job of the controller.

Then someone in the organization should be entrusted with the assignment of observing impartially the progress of the factory we have in mind, from the standpoint of effectiveness generally. This includes appraising the standards and budgets themselves, which have been established by manufacturing management, and, perhaps, reporting on their validity to general management. This again is the work of the controller. He must both earn and be accorded a free hand to make this contribution, that he may do so without offence to his associates and with the assurance of a receptive ear for his findings.

Now, these duties are not accounting duties. They are controllership duties and they contrast sharply with accounting duties, even though a thorough training in cost accounting practice is essential to discharging them. We have been so confused in the early development of controllership by its close affinity to accounting that we have almost come to think of a controller as simply a super-accountant with executive status. Nothing could be farther from the truth, and the sooner we recognize it the better off we all will be.

Within an industrial or commercial organization, a controller is a control officer. He employs accounting techniques for the purpose of accomplishing the control function. The realization of this basic truth is the first step in discerning the contrast between controllership and accounting.

NO OPERATING DECISIONS

It is only a mental exercise to expand the example of the factory which we have just been using to embrace the entire company. The controllership attitude and practice is exactly the same. The essential three-fold nature of the control process does not change, even though the complexities of the problem are multiplied. The controller must first see that the business establishes, through authorized management, a plan for the control of operations. Second, he must measure operating results against that plan and report and interpret this performance to all levels of management. And the third step—the decision and action step—he must leave to line authority, retaining, however, the privilege of commenting on the plan itself, the effectiveness of controls, the efficacy of the standards and any phase of policy, organization structure, or procedures relevant to the control process.

But the controller must not make operating decisions or take operating responsibilities. Let him break this law at his own peril. He must not issue instructions. He must not establish budgets for others. He must not take operating people to task for failure to meet the standards.

Controllership establishes and coordinates a plan for the control of operations, providing all the techniques of control; but operating management must put the plan into effect and make it work. The controller's staff measures performance and interprets operations—always making certain that the same facts, though differing in detail, are reported to all levels of supervision—but responsible management must make the decisions.

The controller sometimes must venture as close to the border line as possible without making the actual decision. His facts and interpretations are frequently so impelling that the decision to be made is obvious. But, regardless of any pressure from operating or general management, he must keep entirely free from actual operating responsibility and refuse to be placed in the position of making decisions. The penalty for infraction is the sacrifice of controllership effectiveness.

THE CONTROLLER MUST CONTROL

We have drawn some distinctions which at first may appear fine, but I hope will some day be firm and bold. I have tried to make it clear that the controller is not an accountant, even though he is responsible for the accounting function, and that he is not an operating manager, even though, in exercising the control function, he contributes to every major management decision.

A proper understanding of these relationships should remove all offensive connotation from the word "control." It should relieve the controller of the accusation of mere personal ambition in giving expression to this control principle, which is his main reason for holding the office.

Let us then recognize frankly that a controller's job is to control. There is nothing ominous about the word, properly understood. Control is a vital, unselfish force which gives a company direction and balance. It is the controller's business to provide this force. It matters little whether his title be controller, treasurer or vice-president, so long as he provides the control machinery, keeps it in working order, and sees that it is properly used by the organization.

Like most mechanical wonders, this machinery is simple in principle. At the risk of repetition, let me say that it consists of (1) a plan, (2) reporting on performance against the plan, and (3) decision and action as indicated. This pattern is repeated as many times as there are units of responsible supervision in the company, and the whole is brought together into a grand plan which directs the company's operations and controls its course.

WHAT IS A CONTROL UNIT?

The typical control unit is the departmental budget, the monthly reporting of actual results compared with budget, and, by process of logic, the resulting action by the department manager, frequently reaching forward to new and better plans and budgets. Multiplied and magnified, this simple mechanism becomes tiller and rudder for the business. The plan embraces sales forecast, operating budgets, a capital expenditure program, a financing plan, a merchandising plan, research and product planning—all fitted into the master plan. Only when this hard, constructive thinking has been done, by all levels of management from the president down, can the planning job be completed.

In this process, we reap a fine harvest. We force ourselves to make decisions in advance, at the proper time, as distinguished from procrastinating until a crisis is upon us. This single benefit will more than pay the salaries of the controller and a liberal staff.

When this mass of planning has been stated by the operating management in terms of dollars, it is a relatively simple task for the controller to prepare a forecast profit and loss statement for a year ahead.

Similarly, a financial program, including pro forma balance sheets for two or three future years, may be constructed. These statements are simply the casting up of all of the planning that has been done. They are the key to understanding the plan. They sometimes indicate adjustments which may have to be made in the plan to make it profitable. But we must forever keep in mind the fact that these statements are not the plan itself. Accounting in this usage must always be subservient to planning and control.

The significant point here is that in order for control to be effective—or, in fact, to come into being at all—there must be a plan. It is the controller's job to see to it that such a plan exists. If his company has been operating on a hand-to-mouth basis, without definitive forward planning, he must accept this challenge and begin the slow process of education which precedes acceptance of the idea.

At the same time, he must remember that control is not susceptible to implementation by the controller alone. His work is done best when it is least mysterious. When the other elements of management use the control technique intelligently and voluntarily, the controller's achievement is greatest. He reaches maximum stature when his contribution is most inconspicuously made, when the planning and control philosophy he cultivates becomes the accepted mode of thought.

In this enlightened sense, let the controller control, and let him never hesitate to assume the responsibilities implied by that word.

PARTICIPATION IN PLANNING

I hope that it has become a little clearer, in the foregoing analysis, that accounting is not the first concern of controllership—that it is essentially a tool with which to shape the mechanisms of control. If you can accept this conclusion, it will naturally follow that the successful controller of the future will be a businessman first and an accountant second. He will have to turn resolutely from his preoccupation with accounting statements and tax returns and think as top management thinks. He must, in fact, consider himself a part of top management.

This transition is not always easy for controllers. Ingrained habits of thought have built for us imaginary signposts, which we follow obediently. When we are asked to participate in a pricing conference, for instance, we say, in effect: "I can furnish all the costs but when it comes to setting selling prices, I have nothing to contribute." Why do we talk like this? Are not the prices of our products as important to profits as manufacturing costs? Or, upon being invited to a meeting on the merchandising of new products, our self-made signposts keep us securely in the road with the deep ruts. We say: "I can turn out reams of figures with my beautiful machines, I can make all sorts of computations, but as for actually helping to construct this plan, that, of course, is out of my line." Why do we thus throw into the discard our best opportunity to contribute to the growth and progress of our companies?

Why do we not cast off the shell of accounting and associate ourselves vitally with the planning process, in order that we may control more intelligently?

There is no phase of a company's operations, policies, or planning that is not the concern of the controller. Everybody's business is his business, assuming he is possessed of the tact and resourcefulness to conduct himself in a way that will bring him the confidence of his associates.

This statement does not in any way conflict with the dictum specified earlier in this paper—that the controller must not himself make decisions. He need never transgress this rule in order to take an active, dynamic part in the planning process. For only the controller is in a position to know exactly what is required for an integrated plan. Only he can visualize adequately the need for planning of product development, manufacturing, purchasing, merchandising, financing—and the final coordination of these segmental plans by translation into a planned net profit.

The very objectives of the business therefore become the controller's concern. He is the man best equipped to attempt an unbiased measure of their validity. He is properly concerned with the effectiveness of all policies adopted by his company, beginning at the point when they are first given consideration. And because effective control is impossible without sound procedures and organization structure, he cannot avoid taking a hand in these also.

EXTERNAL ECONOMICS

There is still another field into which controllership must project itself. The controller must consciously turn his thinking outward to the affairs of the world in which his business lives. No management can afford to ignore the economic factors related to his business. No controller can afford to remain outside a field of thought which has been entered by the president of his company. If he does, he cannot perform the control function effectively, because the objectives of the business are being conditioned by those influences. He cannot appraise the objectives of the business without interpreting the impact thereon of economic, social, and governmental forces.

The most obvious area in which to illustrate this point is the sales forecast. I use this term here interchangeably with "sales budget." By whatever name, it is one of the basic instruments of planning, and should represent the estimate of sales volume to be used for purposes of planning income, production, and profits.

Now, the controller cannot properly establish the company's sales forecast or budget. If he does, either with or without the president's specific approval, it becomes the controller's forecast and not the commitment of the sales department. The sales forecast may be established by the sales organization, by top management or by a management committee, but never by the controller if he hopes to use it as a basis for control.

Nevertheless, he is entitled, and should be required, to express an opinion concerning the forecast. Without doing so he cannot act intelligently as the chief coordinating officer for planning. To perform this task, he must cultivate a sensitiveness to economic currents which will enable him to relate them to the affairs of his company. He must be equipped to interpret these trends with as much facility as those actually responsible for establishing the forecast.

The complexity of the general field of economics and the extent of disagreement among economists combine to make this perhaps the most difficult of the controllership assignments. For a multitude of reasons, it is the one in which procrastination is most evident. Some controllers have attacked it in force, however, and have promptly found it too big for one man to handle. Some companies have employed economists, to consult with all elements of management concerned with forecasting. Others have employed outside consultants in this field. Whatever the method used, the controller has the obligation to bring to the sales forecast his own objective analysis, making use of the best economic talent available.

Like accounting, economics finds its place in the controller's box of tools.

CHIEF ACCOUNTING OFFICER

Among the many duties which have usually fallen to the controller are those of chief accounting officer of the corporation. These are important duties. It is not my purpose to minimize them but rather to put them into focus. Although the core of controllership is the planning and control activity, the controller is asked to do many other things. He is frequently assigned the tasks of office management, insurance administration, treasury administration. Usually he has the position of chief accounting officer, including responsibility for the company's taxes. The last named has sometimes usurped the controller's time and energies to the extent of obscuring his true mission.

Nevertheless, it is right that the controller should number among his assignments those of maintaining the books of account, of handling the company's tax affairs, and of providing internal audit protection. It is proper that he should determine and report the periodic net income and other operating figures, and prepare the balance sheets and other financial data. It is proper too that he be considered the responsible executive with regard to reporting to governmental agencies, a duty which accords closely with his other accounting and tax functions.

In order to carry out the assignment as chief accounting officer without endangering the performance of the planning and control activity, the controller will find two steps indispensable to the proper use of his time. First, he will need to delegate the accounting work—except for the most important policy decisions—to capable assistants, with sufficient authority to perform effectively. And, secondly, he should cultivate the inclination to depend heavily on public accounting for the answers to technical problems concerning determination of income, balance sheet valuations, reserves, methods of stating financial information, and so on.

TAX ADMINISTRATION

Similar reasoning governs the manner in which he handles tax administration. He must never permit himself the too expensive luxury of conducting tax affairs which he could delegate to a tax manager, even though his leaning may be in that direction. And, unless his company is large enough to employ a tax staff of high calibre, he ought to rely on the kind of tax consulting service that recognized public accounting firms can offer, in order to take advantage of their broader experience in this field. He is then free to devote his efforts to making certain that in the early stages of each business decision, ample thought is given to its tax implications. This is one of the very profitable but frequently neglected opportunities.

Having made these arrangements, the controller may, as the occasion arises, certify his income statements and balance sheets for whatever purposes may require his certification—whether for governmental agencies or his own board of directors. He may affix his signature to tax returns as chief accounting officer, with the confidence that they are as nearly correct as he himself could make them. And as for his accounting figures, both he and his board of directors are entitled to the protection and the independent point of view which can only be secured through an independent annual audit by a recognized public accounting firm. Following this pattern, we may say that the controller discharges his obligation as chief accounting officer without sacrificing the vital planning and control functions.

THE INDUSTRIAL ACCOUNTANT

I have tried to draw a line between controllership and accounting, because it is my conviction that confusing the two has been detrimental to the progress of both. It has retarded controllership because corporate managements have tended to think of controllers primarily as accounting executives concerned largely with preparing statements and tax returns. It has retarded accounting because in trying to treat the newer controllership science as one of its branches, accounting has become overextended.

What about the accountant in private industry? Have I left him out of this picture of mutual usefulness and respect? I contend that he is in no way

43

slighted by these concepts. Let him simply recognize that his work is essentially control, and that all of the finely polished techniques of accounting which he has studied and practiced so well are pointed in that direction. Whether he be a budget accountant, a cost accountant, or a general accountant, his horizons will be broader and his effectiveness increased if he will fix his eyes on the controllership idea. His work is indispensable to its fulfillment.

Obviously, there are administrative and record-keeping duties to be performed which are not planning and control activities. There are books to post, bills to pay, invoices to make, tax returns to file, statements to prepare, and countless other accounting and related duties to perform. They are important, but they are not controllership. The industrial accountant will do well to remember that the only channels leading to controllership are those assignments partaking in some degree of the planning and control process. The industrial accountant who wishes to progress would also do well to ask himself whether the controller of his company has a progressive concept of controllership, which is the climate most conducive to growth for the controller's staff.

DEFINITION OF CONTROLLERSHIP

The concept of controllership which we have been discussing is not new. It has been developing in this line for quite a few years. It is revolutionary, however, if we compare it with the attitude prevalent 20 years ago, and revolutionary ideas sometimes take hold slowly.

A few years ago the Controllers Institute of America officially recognized the need for establishing a concept of controllership which would do justice to its current state of development and set a standard for controllers to follow. The task was assigned to a committee and, after long and careful work, a statement of the Institute's concept of the function of controllership was approved by the National Board of Directors on September 25, 1949.

I should like to invite you to examine this statement in the light of our discussion. You will notice in its six parts a subordination of accounting techniques and practice to the major elements of planning and control. The function of controllership, as stated by the Institute, [*appears in Exhibit 1 on page 18*].

If this definition were applied literally and universally, business would reap untold benefits. The presence of the controllership force in a company releases the energies of its operating management and of its chief executive to carry out their assignments more effectively. Properly exercised, controllership stabilizes management thinking and provides firm guidance to all levels of the organization. It adds a harmonizing influence to the councils of management—always objective, always deeply concerned with ferreting out the truth of every situation, unfailingly generous and impartial. Only with this attitude can controllership be practiced successfully.

ROAD-BLOCKS AHEAD

But we must face the fact that controllership has a long road to travel before it is practiced universally according to the Institute's definition. One reason for this is the confusion with accounting that I have referred to so frequently in this paper. This problem is widespread and permeates the thinking of presidents and controllers alike. When we have established our distinction, we shall have cleared the way for further progress.

Another road-block is a peculiar misconception harbored by controllers themselves. Many of us seem to think that in assuming the responsibilities listed we are in some way usurping the prerogatives of the president of the company. When the proper attitude is understood and evidenced, this objection will evaporate. It is the controller's absolute adherence to the enumerated principles which accomplishes this result. It is the patient, persevering habit of giving freely of his best efforts, of stating truth fearlessly, of contributing with unselfish motives to the effectiveness and achievement of other executives, without claiming credit for himself. When we have mastered these precepts, we shall control without malice and without fear of being misunderstood.

A third obstacle is the tendency for controllers to abdicate their responsibilities. Frequently we imply that we have no concern with planning, with the broad objectives of the business, or with economic developments, because these are assigned to others in the organization. This is a matter for gradual growth, both in the controllership idea and in the individual practitioner. Adopting a modern, tested concept, we can, by study and self-training, encourage our thinking and our conversation to move naturally in the desired direction. Ultimately, if our principle is sound and our practice honest, we shall have the visible manifestation of our progress.

Other causes of failure come to mind, perhaps as a result of those just mentioned. For instance, controllers often fancy themselves too busy to get at the real task to be done. They permit themselves a chronic overload of work, most of which misses the main target. They are absorbed in daily administration, in laying out accounting systems, in writing instruction manuals—in everything that prevents their promoting the use of planning and control principles. Controllers as a group must cease their senseless preoccupation with tabulating machines and bookkeeping systems. These duties can be successfully delegated. The construction of a control system usually cannot.

THE ROAD AHEAD

Probably no one can predict the future of controllership today. It is fairly safe to say that it is still in its growing stages. Sales management, manufacturing, purchasing and, more recently, personnel relations have blossomed into major areas in the science of management. All are better understood than this newcomer.

We have an important work before us. The principles and rules of this science must be made widely known. Our planning techniques must be made more definitive. Our forecasting and budgeting must be more clearly understood. These tasks cannot be escaped if we are to have "everything under control."

To accomplish this task, controllers must understand controllership. Accountants must also understand controllership in order that their relation to it and their part in it may be clear. For accounting and controllership always will rely heavily on each other. Though separate, they are mutually interdependent.

Controllership is not properly taught in our universities today because the faculties do not understand its fundamentals. They insist on treating it as a development of managerial accounting. This is solely our fault. We must teach the schools before they can be expected to teach the students. Some day it will be seen that courses in controllership belong in university departments of management rather than in departments of accounting.

Nothing in this paper detracts from or criticizes the accounting fraternity, for which I have the deepest respect. I hope I have made it clear that for controllership to stand on its own feet, as a part of management, with the controller placed as staff to the chief executive in every business, and for accounting to serve them both, can only augment the well-deserved praises already bestowed on the accounting profession.

Controllership, geared to embrace every phase of a company's operations with its planning and control principles, is fraught with opportunity and inspiration. Its march of progress cannot be stopped. Wider recognition is being given the organization status of controllers, as specified by the Controllers Institute of America—"an executive officer at the policy-making level responsible directly to the chief executive officer of the business." With the concepts of management now emerging, and based on a clear understanding of its field of action, controllership can make hitherto undreamed-of contributions to the advancement of industry.

To see this fruition, we must all keep our thinking straight. We must study the principles of controllership, practice them well, and keep our own ships on the course, just as our control methods aim to do for our companies.

THE PLANNING AND CONTROL CONCEPT †

by
James L. Peirce

A discussion of the planning and control idea might be started by saying that it is synonymous with management itself. Certainly no business can exist without some form of this twin concept, and it might perhaps be demonstrated that success in business is proportionate to the astuteness of its planning and the skill with which it is controlled.

This sweeping statement, however, would dodge the important issues. Although business has lived through many decades of history with marked success, the full planning and control principle is only now emerging and gaining acceptance. This concept can now be reduced to precepts and rules, which may be followed with predictable results. As a consequence, planning, deliberate and detailed, has assumed a new priority among the duties of management at all levels; and controllership, which is the orderly practice of control in business, has become a profitable branch of the science of management.

DEFINITION OF PLANNING

It may be useful at the outset to define "planning" (as the word is understood in the concept we are discussing) and to place it in relation to the control function. Planning, of course, is carried on during every hour of the business day, and sometimes during many other hours besides. It may exist with or without control—that is, with or without disciplined efforts to follow the plan or to explain deviations from it. On the other hand, control cannot exist without planning, and therefore the planning must be designed to fit the specifications of control.

In the modern sense of an integrated planning and control system, then, planning refers to the construction of an operating program, comprehensive enough to cover all phases of operations, and detailed enough that specific attention may be given to its fulfillment in controllable segments. It may therefore be reiterated that the planning process must be conducted in direct relation to the needs of control.

†Reprinted from *The Controller*, September 1954, pp. 403-406, 422, 424-425, copyright 1954, with permission of the Financial Executives Institute, 10 Madison Avenue, P.O. Box 1938, Morristown, NJ 07962-1938. (201) 898-4600.

DEFINITION OF CONTROL

An examination of this word "control" shows that, like many another word in the English language, it has a number of meanings. It is absolutely necessary to have a clear understanding of its definition in the specialized sense in which it will be used herein.

Perhaps the easiest approach to this shade of meaning is to mention some of the things that the word "control" in this usage does not include. It does not signify the kind of control over a business enjoyed by a majority shareholder. It does not refer to any part of the control centered in a board of directors or a president. It does not include line authority for making or carrying out policy or operating decisions.

When then is "control" in the sense to be used here? It is defined as the presence in a business of that force which guides it to a predetermined objective by means of predetermined policies and decisions. Every business executive can identify this control force in his company. It operates quite apart from the mass of operating decisions and instructions constantly emanating from the line organization. It does not steer the course but it informs operating management at once of any significant deviation from it. It does not take action, but it frequently impels action by turning a spotlight on the pertinent facts.

ORGANIZATION ASPECTS

The practice of this variety of control may be referred to as controllership. When delegated, it is exercised by an executive properly called a controller, although he may not actually carry that title. His title may be, for example, vice president and treasurer and his controllership assignment intermingled with financial and other administrative duties. Nevertheless, regardless of title, because he performs the controllership function, he will be referred to here as the controller.

The problem of assignment and performance of duties in the organization structure will be touched upon at a subsequent point in this paper. For the purpose of delineating the planning and control concept, it may be summarized in this way: Planning is the primary duty of the president, assisted by all line and staff executives. The control function is exercised by the same group, but may be centered functionally in the controller. The objective of controllership is to assist all levels of management in controlling to the plan. It never issues orders, but it coordinates the machinery of planning, records and reveals the facts and makes plain to those in charge what they must do to achieve the prescribed aim.

THE CONTROL FORMULA

The control process, like all effective modes of management, rests on a simple principle. It may be stated as a three-part formula:

The first component is the adoption of a plan.

The second is reporting actual performance as compared with the plan.

The third is making decisions and taking action.

This pattern is repeated as many times as there are units of responsible supervision in the company, and the whole is assembled as a grand plan which directs the company's operations and controls its course. As time goes on, experience sometimes dictates alterations in the plan. Action taken as a result of reporting performance against plan reaches forward to new and better plans.

It should be evident that the three phases of the formula are operating concurrently—that a management following this system will be constantly planning, reporting and taking action. The important thing to note is that the decisions reached and the actions taken will be directly related to a master plan. They will not be spasmodic nor will they be consummated without adequate reference to the fundamental objectives of the business. No decision or action will be taken which is out of harmony with actions in other departments of the business, because all are governed by a universal plan.

To accomplish this atmosphere of controlled power requires diligent effort by men who are both fully conscious of the importance of this technique and willing to accept the self-discipline that it requires.

THE ADOPTION OF THE PLAN

The initial step, the adoption of a plan, is perhaps the most difficult. Even after the habit of planning has become ingrained, it is not easy to induce a group of executives to set aside pressing matters and think into the problematical future. Perhaps this step can only be accomplished through the firm insistence of the president, combined with the monotonous persistence of the controller.

First, consider the form in which the planning is to be stated. The common denominator, of course, is money. All planning must ultimately be translated into dollar figures, which is the language in which business operates. The ultimate form of the programming therefore is, typically, a planned profit-and-loss statement for a forthcoming period of, say, 12 months, supported in detail by sales budgets or forecasts, expense budgets and so on, and also supplemented with detailed explanations. The assumptions, bases and computations upon which the budget figures are predicated all should be recorded because they will later serve a vital purpose.

These figures are not the plan itself. They are only the external expression of the plan, in a language understandable to all. The statements are a mere vehicle with which to inform, appraise and perchance readjust. The substance of the plan itself is in the minds of its creators.

It would hardly be necessary to emphasize this self-evident truth if it were not ignored so often. It is of no value whatever to budget a given amount for advertising, for instance, without clear advance knowledge on the part of the advertising manager of the media to be used, the markets to be reached, the products to be advertised. In fact, the advertising budget does not qualify as a segment of a true operating plan unless the sales manager also understands the exact degree of support it will afford him in selling his forecast volume.

Let no one be satisfied with a mere estimate, offered without detailed study and based on nothing more than last year's expenditures. Though purporting to be an advertising budget, it is actually only a guess, lacking in supporting reasoning, subject to manipulation and devoid of responsibility.

To be effective, planning cannot be superficial. It depends on a firm statement of principles by the top executive, a clear understanding by each man of the contribution his division or department is expected to make to the enterprise, and a willingness to plan with care and to stand back of the plan. An expense budget, for example, reflecting the planning of an individual unit of the business, must be prepared with utter sincerity, and with a commitment to follow the charted course or stand accountable for any substantial deviation.

WHAT THE PLAN COVERS

Anyone who has taken part in the preparation of a plan of operations for an industrial company is aware that the undertaking is far more comprehensive than it may first appear. No activity of the company is exempt; every segment must be fitted into a master program.

Consider for a moment the implications of preparing a sales budget, sometimes referred to as a sales forecast, for a period of a year ahead. All products must be budgeted, including those which have not yet been introduced. Due weight must be given the general economic outlook and its bearing on the demand for the company's products. The effect on volume of proposed changes in merchandising methods must be considered. Both volume and selling prices must be planned, and this involves an advance determination of the quantities to be sold in each market or through each sales outlet.

Bear in mind that creative sales budgeting will not tolerate retrospection, astrology nor guesswork. The penalties are too severe. For example, the sales promotion budget will lean heavily on the planned sales volume. What is perhaps even more significant, so will factory production levels, purchase commitments and the ever-critical acquisition and layoff of production workers. Planning is a company-wide process of integration, in which no man can stand alone. All depend upon each other.

When the volume of planned sales has been established, the manufacturing division is in a position to plan production levels and times, as well as inventories. Manufacturing costs must then be fitted into the program, including material purchase prices, wage levels and even manufacturing efficiency. The planning process then fans out to include factory administration costs, research objectives, selling strategy and general administration. The spotlight is turned on the future course of each activity and each is reduced to budgeted figures.

Finally, when all this planning has been done and translated into the language of dollars—after financing decisions have been made and estimates of money costs and income taxes prepared—it is possible to arrive at the planned net profit. It is this figure which determines return on the capital invested in the business and willingness on the part of investors to provide more capital as required by its growth.

It is this figure also which has such a marked effect on the prosperity of the business that it becomes the key point in the planning process. If it is deficient, it must be raised. And it can only be raised, normally, in one of two ways: an increase in planned sales income or a decrease in budgeted outgo. The adjustment at this critical point may involve major revision of important segments of the plan, reaching back once more into the deep recesses of the thinking of all elements of management.

PLANNING IS A MAN-SIZED JOB

We have skimmed lightly over a process which sometimes taxes the capacity and judgment of every executive in the business. It is not an easy task to make major operating decisions for 12 months ahead and place them neatly on a timetable. Yet this is what must be done if the company is to operate under the kind of control that produces satisfactory results.

Suppose, for example, that you are a general sales manager. You are asked by the controller for a budget of sales volume and expense for the coming year—the first three months separately and the remainder of the year by quarters. This is a fairly common way to make a budget. You pinpoint the period immediately ahead but are not asked to be quite so accurate in timing the remainder of the year.

You know from experience that you have to do a good job in preparing this plan—not because you will be fired if you do not meet it, but because the actions of so many other people are geared to your planning. You also know that there are going to be a lot of explanations to make if your actual performance is not according to plan. So you resolve to plan very carefully and insist that your subordinates do likewise with respect to their parts of the process.

But the first thing you stumble on is a new product shortly to be released by the research division. You explain to the controller that the research director does not know exactly when the item will be ready; it may be in six months or it may take 12, depending upon what priority can be given it in the research division program. So, of course, your first inclination is to feel that you cannot be responsible for a sales forecast under these circumstances.

Furthermore, the ripples from this problem affect the timing of your space advertising insertions. Not until you have definite knowledge on a release date for the product will you be in a position to turn loose a barrage of direct mail promotion. Then you discover that certain traveling and sales training expenses also depend directly on the introduction date of this product. As a result your entire budget is tentative and uncertain.

You explain all this to the controller, but he is not very sympathetic. He simply says that you will be held responsible for your forecast and budget, and if you have no definite information on release dates for new products, it will be necessary to get them. But, he offers to help you to find the answers. This results in a conference with the president and the research director, in which agreement is reached as to completion date for the project; but you then discover that the manufacturing group will require additional time for production of tools and rearrangement of factory layout before the first units can be finished, and that purchasing requires time to obtain material commitments.

DIVIDENDS FROM THE DIFFICULTIES

After a difficult series of conferences, during which all product planning is given a searching review, a conclusion is reached, in which all concur, as to a release date for the new product. You then proceed to complete your budget.

Perhaps this typical incident will afford a hint of the constructive power released by the planning and control mechanism. Nothing short of a conscious policy and formal channels for the process to follow could force the hard thinking which leads to advance decisions on such knotty problems as the one described. To paraphrase a familiar anecdote—"Many decisions which are impossible to make simply take a little longer."

Sometimes these advance determinations are subject to subsequent revision. The planning process should accommodate this need. If decisions must be made subject to probable change, all concerned should understand the assumptions on which they are based and the extent to which the plan may have to be altered. Flexibility, not rigidity, is a characteristic of dynamic planning.

The dividend from this process is proportionate to the magnitude of the hurdles surmounted. First, there is time for deliberation on the problems appearing on the horizon, as contrasted with solving them at the last minute in an atmosphere of crisis. And second, the kind of interchange described in the foregoing illustration yields a mutual understanding of the basics of the business which could not be obtained in any other way. There is no comparable training course for executives.

CAPITAL EXPENDITURE PLANNING

Planning of the company's operations cannot be considered complete unless it is integrated with a plan for providing required new buildings, machinery, equipment, tools and so on. The needs of the organization in this area should be assembled as carefully as are the departmental operating budgets.

In this case, however, the term of planning is usually a little longer—say three years, as compared with the customary 12-month projection of sales and expenses. Capital requirements must be prepared on a long-range basis because of the time requirement for construction and procurement and because these items are largely charged against the income of future years.

Furthermore, such expenditures will largely govern the planning for financing. The logical outcome of this thinking is a phase of planning which is far broader than capital expenditures alone, and which might be referred to as a financial program.

In constructing such a program, estimates must be made of required operating cash, accounts receivable and inventories, as well as plant and equipment items for the planned period. In fact, every item on the company's balance sheet receives scrutiny in this process, and the resulting financial program may be expressed in terms of pro forma balance sheets for each of the succeeding three years. Obviously, borrowings, net profits, dividends and enlistments of new equity capital must be planned in order to accomplish this result.

The process of constructing a financial program is perhaps even more difficult than that of creating an operating plan for a one-year period. It requires that proposed major moves be frozen into at least tentative decisions, which can usually be made only by boards of directors.

The benefits of such programming are proportionate to its cost, however, and correspond to those adduced to operating planning. Objectives are defined. Decisions are reached in advance. A course is set. Furthermore, it is a comfortable feeling to know that so long as the company is able to follow the plan, it will not suddenly be faced with a shortage of cash some morning, with little or no warning.

REPORTING ON PERFORMANCE

It will be recalled that the control formula consists of (1) the adoption of a plan, (2) reporting actual performance as compared with the plan, and (3) making decisions and taking action. The second of these steps merits a brief discussion.

Probably the simplest known form of reporting performance against plan is the typical expense report issued by the accounting department, showing itemized expenses for the month, compared with budget figures. Too often the reporting ends there. It should add two other features: a written explanation of the figure where it would be helpful, and sympathetic consultation with the recipient of the figures. The latter should only be lengthy enough to ascertain that the man responsible really understands the meaning of the figures.

The same principle, of course, applies to profit-and-loss statements and to reporting on the performance of any unit of the business. The reporting cannot be perfunctory. It must be based on an intimate knowledge of the operation and of the plan itself, rather than merely on the figures. For instance, it is far more significant to point out a deviation from a planned expansion of the sales force than to report only that salaries are so many dollars less than the amount budgeted.

In all cases, the controller must get at the essential facts. He must report the same story to all levels of supervision involved. And he must take the responsibility for seeing that the facts are not only reported but understood. The hard core of the reporting is comparison of actual with planned performance, in sufficient detail that every fraction of the operation, and thereby the whole, may be controlled.

DECISION AND ACTION

The final step in the control formula is decision and action. When the planning has been done properly and adequate reporting has been made on performance against the plan, the ensuing decisions sometimes become surprisingly clear. The action is frequently indicated in the reporting itself.

Assume, for example, a failure of actual manufacturing cost to match the planned cost for a given month. The result, of course, shows up in a deficient net profit. The excess of actual over budgeted or planned cost has been traced to its source. It is relatively easy to do this if the plan has been constructed in adequate detail by the manufacturing organization.

Whether the reason be low production volume, high material prices, heavy waste losses, or any of the myriad of other happenings which push costs upward, management is faced at once with a clear-cut decision. Either the condition must be corrected, or, if this is not possible, other changes in the plan must be made to compensate for it. Planned expenses, costs or sales volume must be improved, or planned net profit must be reduced.

The decision should be reached in an atmosphere of participation by everyone concerned. If an adjustment is made in the plan itself, each responsible executive and supervisor accepts the full impact of the change on the performance expected of him.

In practice, an orderly method is required for revision of the operating plan and reflection of the change in the projected operating figures. For example, it may be advisable to give effect to new planning and changes in plan only at three-month intervals, in the course of a complete revision of budgets. Interim deviations, meanwhile, are made conspicuous, in harmony with the best management-by-exception tradition.

By these devices of control, all units of the business are coordinated. The simple triad, planning-reporting-action, becomes the guiding principle of the business. When this state of thinking has permeated the organization—when this *modus operandi* has become second nature—management potential reaches a new altitude and the business responds with superior performance.

WHO IS RESPONSIBLE?

It is a long step from the resolution to have better planning and control to its actual realization. As in every other advance in management method, responsibility must be fixed at the outset. In this case, however, the assignment of responsibility is decidedly complex.

Fundamentally, every manager or supervisor in charge of a unit of the business well enough defined to have a budget of its own must be made responsible for the planning and control of that unit. By implication, the responsibility travels up the organization line all the way to the top.

The president, of course, is ultimately charged with the obligation of success in this field, as in all others, and he therefore must undertake to see that the control mechanism is constructed and maintained and that the entire organization is educated in its use.

Because this multiple task is so time consuming, experience has proven the wisdom of assigning it to a staff executive who may be referred to as the controller. The latter, if he is alert to the immense possibilities of the planning and control concept, and aware that he is the executive in the most advantageous position to carry out the assignment, will need to reorganize his thinking, and perhaps his entire department. He will need to subordinate all accounting, cost and budget activities to the needs of the greater sphere of planning and control.

Essentially the burden of installation, education and follow-up falls on the president and the controller. The respective areas of action of these two executives require a little further comment.

THE PRESIDENT'S RESPONSIBILITY

It is axiomatic that all policies of management must enjoy the unqualified support of the top man in the business. Planning and control techniques are no exception. The company's president must understand them, use them himself and furnish the required leadership in their application.

This philosophy permeates through the organization only when the president gives it being and vitality. If his allegiance to it is lukewarm, his adherence tentative and his concept hazy, he cannot expect his controller to keep it alive and vigorous. It might be possible to operate a passable control system without a controller, if the president were equal to the task. The reverse, however, is not true. No controller can accomplish it without the wholehearted and intelligent collaboration of the chief executive of the business.

It is probably self-evident that the same comments apply, in degree, to executive vice presidents, division and department managers and others. The acceptance and use of the planning and control concept must be commensurate with the authority invested. It is the president's task to create an understanding of these points in his immediate subordinates, who in turn are held accountable for transmitting this understanding and making control effective throughout their respective spheres of activity.

THE CONTROLLER'S RESPONSIBILITY

It should be re-emphasized that the control function, within the concept we are discussing is not always assigned to an executive with the title of controller. It is frequently found to reside in a top financial or administrative officer, and sometimes remains in the hands of the chief executive. Perhaps it would be clearer to refer to the duties of controllership, regardless of where they are vested.

Nevertheless, more and more business management is turning to a concept which provides a controller for the business, delegates to him the duties of controllership in the modern sense, and relieves him of operating duties. It does not relieve him of various functions traditionally associated with that office, such as those of chief accounting officer or the responsibility for tax administration, internal auditing and sometimes credit, insurance and office management. Nevertheless, these duties should be subordinate to the compelling task of providing effective controls for the business. Accounting in particular, long considered the major concern of controllers, fits into its proper place as a tool of control.

DEFINITION OF CONTROLLERSHIP

As defined by the Controllers Institute of America [*Editors' Note: see Exhibit 1 on page 18*], the functions of controllership include establishing, coordinating and maintaining an integrated plan for the control of operations, but it is specified that this must be done through authorized management. Such a plan, it is stated, would provide cost standards, expense budgets, sales forecasts, profit planning and programs for capital investment and financing, together with the necessary procedures to effectuate the plan. The important words in this assignment are "through authorized management" and this little phrase sets the keynote for the controller's peculiar mode of getting things accomplished. He himself should never establish a single standard or budget (except his own), nor a single sales forecast. The plan must be constructed, under his helpful guidance, by the operating executives who will have to accept the responsibility for performance.

The Institute's definition then assigns to the controller the duty of measuring performance against approved operating plans and standards, and of reporting and interpreting the results of operations to all levels of management. It is within this assignment that he finds the need for designing, installing and maintaining accounting and cost systems and records, determining accounting policy and compiling statistics.

Other parts of the definition equip the controller with power to measure, interpret and report on almost anything—even the validity of the objectives of the business—and to consult with all responsible segments of management on any phase of the operation of the business. He is also charged with the duty of interpreting economic and social influences in their impact on the business. He is free, in fact, to offer his constructive thinking wherever he feels that it will contribute to more effective planning, direction, control.

A discreet controller can exercise this wide latitude without offense to his fellow executives, provided he heeds the ground rules of controllership. These include a fastidious abstention from taking on operating responsibilities or making operating decisions; reporting consistently to all concerned; insisting that the line organization determine their own budgets and standards of performance; and above all, reporting and interpreting without exaggeration, bias or regard for the preconceptions of others.

In particular also, he must not take operating people to task for failure to meet the standards, and he must not be placed in the position of making negative decisions on spending money. It is a familiar myth that these unpleasant attributes are the characteristics of a controller. The penalty for permitting this misconception to be accepted among his associates is the sacrifice of controllership effectiveness.

The particular state of mind that the controller ought to impart to the organization is a sense of balance, stability and direction.

THE ROAD AHEAD

It would be unfortunate to leave the impression that planning and control solve all the problems of running a business. Planning and control simply facilitate the solution of these problems very materially and open up possibilities of achievement which could not be realized otherwise. In a word, it represents thinking forward instead of meeting each daily crisis when it arises. It represents detailed knowledge of where and why we are going astray, as contrasted with a tardy awakening to developments which have been buried for too long in the debris of current affairs. Its fruition is a priceless sense of knowing where we are going rather than steering a blind course.

The question may be asked: What do you do when your planning has all been carefully arranged, your control system is working smoothly, and you suddenly encounter some unforeseeable disaster, such as a strike? Plans are completely upset, decisions made hand-to-mouth. The situation is analogous to that of a ship in a storm. You do not dispense with the instruments of navigation. You simply reconcile yourself to the fact that they are momentarily less effective, and re-establish your course as soon as possible. There is nothing about an emergency that lessens the need for planning and control. On the contrary, the effect of the crisis, the means for meeting it and the measures required to repair the damage are all appraised more accurately and quickly in relation to an established plan.

If clear direction is needed to surmount the difficulties of the years to come, then there must be orderly thinking. All units of the business must be brought into harmony. The complex specializations demanded of the various departments must be synchronized so that the whole may move forward together more confidently.

This is a present possibility. We are just beginning to learn the unlimited benefits of wisely conducted planning and of control constructively applied. New and better methods will constantly improve the practice of planning and control, but its unchanging principles, symbolized by the planning-reporting-action formula, are the eternal possession of business management from the time of their discovery.

CONTROLLERSHIP AND COST ACCOUNTING [†]

by

James L. Peirce

THE more one thinks about the subject of controllership in its particular relationship to cost accounting the more he is convinced that it is a subject laden with misconceptions awaiting the touch of truth that they may be annihilated.

Now such a situation cannot exist without also being fraught with opportunity for all who face it. In this case the challenge is very clear indeed, and accepting it is accompanied by a kind of exhilaration, even though we may at this time do no more than strike the first blow in a long battle.

One thing must be made clear at the outset. We are fighting misconceptions—not people or professions. No one can rightly contemplate the achievements of the cost accountants with less than profound admiration. To focus attention on its unique service relationship to controllership—in which both sciences, if they may be so called, cultivate an identical approach to the control aspects of business—can only result in a greater general appreciation of each. For each has its own distinct individuality.

It is especially interesting, I think, to discuss the partnership of controllership with the branch of accounting known as cost accounting, not only because the relationship of controllership and general accounting has been more completely explored in recent literature, but because it has always seemed to me that controllership is closer to cost accounting.

This presupposes several things, with which you may or may not agree. It first assumes that cost accounting and general accounting are separable areas of thought. I am not by any means certain that this is true. Perhaps each is an extension of the other, and both are phases of the same subject. But if we adopt the view that they may be distinguished from each other, then I feel that cost accounting must be the first love of every controller, because it does more for him than any other field of trained thought in exercising that peculiar force known as control.

[†]Presented before the Chicago Chapter, National Association of Cost Accountants (NACA). Reprinted from *The Controller*, August 1956, pp. 359-361, 384-386, copyright 1956, with permission of the Financial Executives Institute, 10 Madison Avenue, P.O. Box 1938, Morristown, NJ 07962-1938. (201) 898-4600.

DISTINCTIONS AND DEFINITIONS

This hypothesis also presupposes knowledge of what controllership is, of what general accounting is, and of what cost accounting is. The last two named, being older, stand forth more clearly than does controllership. For our purposes, perhaps I can be forgiven for oversimplifying a little, and if so we might say that general accounting is basically concerned with determination of periodic net income and with current financial position. Cost accounting, on the other hand, is essentially engaged in breaking the elements of cost into manageable segments—product costs or budget units, for example—permitting the control of costs and the coordination of costs with selling prices and thereby with profits.

Now controllership is the scientific application of the principles of planning and control to a business to the end that it may grow and prosper. These principles can be stated in pretty clear terms. They represent a directed force within the business that insures its profitability. They call for the most precise tools available and the first to be named is the applied technique of cost accounting, in the broad meaning of that term—in the meaning that covers every income-producing and cost-incurring activity of the business.

If we are to look at the business scene impartially, we must recognize that not all controllers seem entirely sympathetic to this viewpoint. In many cases they are preoccupied with the fascinating problems of net income reporting and with the perennial effort to minimize taxes. Too frequently cost accounting is considered a technique the usefulness of which is confined to the factory, whereas it is actually a trained condition of thought which should be focused on all phases of operations. This situation is changing rapidly, however, and, in any case, we are mostly concerned with conditions as they should be rather than with the places where the light has not yet shone.

To pursue our line of reasoning further, controllership and cost accounting have a definable relationship to each other. It is controllership's mission to establish and maintain proper planning of operations and to control operations in accordance with the plan. It is the assignment of cost accounting to provide the means for fulfilling this main controllership function. Control is the end and cost accounting with its highly refined techniques is the means.

WHAT DOES A CONTROLLER DO?

Before we can really understand the relationship of these two cousins we must first see what controllership looks like. It is surprising how relatively few people really know what a controller is supposed to do. Everyone, beginning with your own secretary, knows what a sales manager or a production manager is responsible for—in a general way at least—but even the controller himself is often found to be in the dark when it comes to defining his own duties properly. Nearly all layers of the business organization think of him as an accountant who has graduated into executive duties, in which his main concern is the administration of the company's accounting responsibilities.

I would like to ask you to set aside this picture long enough to examine with me a more advanced concept of the job. Sooner or later, each one of us is going to be forced to do this very thing if we are to keep up with the management parade. This task is not easy for controllers themselves. Weaned on accounting, they tend to love it and to cling to it. The force of progress is unrelentingly demanding that they now think in terms of planning and control first, and of their beloved accounting techniques as a mode of accomplishing a planned and controlled operation.

THE PLANNING ACTIVITY

At the outset, may I ask that you give a moment's thought to a portion of the statement of the controllership function as published by the Controllers Institute of America. This statement was first issued by the Institute in 1949 and it has steadily grown in prestige since that time. Its first pronouncement is that the controller is expected

> To establish, coordinate and maintain, through authorized management, an integrated plan for the control of operations. Such a plan would provide, to the extent required in the business, cost standards, expense budgets, sales forecasts, profit planning, and programs for capital investment and financing, together with the necessary procedures to effectuate the plan.

I should like to take this first function apart and examine it very briefly—for here is the essence of what controllership must do if business is to survive the twin challenges of automation, with its mounting capital investment, and competition, with its squeeze on the profits which provide the needed capital.

Note first that the controller works entirely "through authorized management" in establishing a plan for the control of operations. Like all other staff people, he does not issue orders. He operates by indirection—creating the plan in such a manner that responsible line management, in theory and in fact, does its own planning. The controller simply sees that the plan is established, coordinated and maintained.

Now note what the plan must provide—cost standards, for example, and expense budgets and sales forecasts—all complete with procedures to make them work. The controller and his staff do not set the cost standards; they simply furnish an effective plan whereby such standards will be established by line management. They are then charged with the responsibility of making the planning operate "through authorized management." And bear in mind that the cost standards so used are only one segment of the master plan which covers the operations of the entire company, even including its program for capital investment and financing.

THE CONTROL ACTIVITY

Let us advance to the second stated function of controllership, which is

To measure performance against approved operating plans and standards, and to report and interpret the results of operations to all levels of management. This function includes the design, installation and maintenance of accounting and cost systems and records, the determination of accounting policy and the compilation of statistical records as required.

Having set up a plan for the control of operations, the controller is now charged with responsibility for measuring performance against the plan and for reporting and interpreting operating results. Note again the subordination of the techniques of accounting to the principal objective. All cost work, along with the maintenance of accounting systems, is directed toward providing the most elaborate fountain of information ever designed by industry—the outpouring of facts from the controller's department.

Note here that the highest level of achievement demands a plan against which to measure, but that even in the absence of formal planning the controller is asked to report and interpret the results of operations. Note too that this reporting is addressed impartially to all levels of management—a clear instruction to report fairly and consistently the same facts to both the responsible man and his boss.

All the minutiae of accounting work, all the prerogatives of accounting policy determination with their undeniable influence on the course of business operation, fall into this pattern. This is the purpose of all cost theory and record keeping—that management may understand its plan, know how it is performing, and reap the benefit of the objective analysis provided by the controller's staff.

I have touched on those functions of the controller which form the foundation of his work—those related to planning, measuring performance, reporting and interpreting. Not only are these fundamental but, for reasons which are by no means coincidental, they are also the functions most intimately connected with cost accounting. I should like to discuss this peculiar kinship a little later, but it seems appropriate first to complete the portrait of controllership by mentioning its other responsibilities, even though they do not relate directly to the subject.

THE INDEPENDENT APPRAISAL ACTIVITY

In the third of the stated functions, Controllers Institute has gone to the heart of the management need for independent appraisal. It says that the controller is obligated

> To measure and report on the validity of the objectives of the business and on the effectiveness of its policies, organization structure and procedures in attaining those objectives. This includes consulting with all segments of management responsible for policy or action concerning any phase of the operation of the business as it relates to the performance of this function.

Now this duty is very broad indeed, and if the wording just quoted happens to be new to you, it may require a little reflection. Perhaps these conclusions will emerge for you as they have for me: (1) that most business is badly in need of intelligent work in this direction; (2) that it is possible for the controller to discharge this function if it is understandingly delegated by top management; (3) that this duty is a natural outgrowth of the controller's other duties; (4) that its discharge in a judicious way does not usurp anyone's prerogatives; and (5) that no other executive, generally speaking, can possess the cultivated objectivity required for this task.

The implications of this opportunity I believe hold special meaning for cost accountants. Not only will many of them become controllers one day and hence be faced with this ultimate test of full controllership activity, but cost accounting itself deserves the broadest possible mental platform. Cost accountants should be thinking and talking management policy, management objectives and management methods. Only in this way can cost accounting fulfill its unlimited possibilities as a management weapon in the assault on today's competitive markets.

OTHER CONTROLLERSHIP ACTIVITIES

The fourth function is

> To report to government agencies, as required, and to supervise all matters relating to taxes.

This is one of the better-known duties of controllers and hardly deserves comment here, but the fifth is still full of unexplored territory. It calls on the controller

> To interpret and report on the effect of external influences on the attainment of the objectives of the business. This function includes the continuous appraisal of economic and social forces and of governmental influences as they affect the operations of the business.

Again I think it may be said that this function is an outgrowth of the others, and indispensable for a complete range of action. No controller's appraisal of a sales department's forecast, for example, would be worth its salt without a knowledge of the interplay of economic forces. No comment on the aims of the business or its progress in fulfilling them could have the ring of validity unless it were backed with a solid understanding of the forces which make the outside world what it is.

This is one of the most neglected fields of thought among accountants and controllers. It may at first seem unrelated to the daily work of cost control, cost finding and communication of cost information, but the contrary is true. If the cost accountant sharpens his intelligence in the field of external economics rather than letting it grow rusty, his penetration into the field of management will be quicker and more certain.

The sixth function is

> To provide protection for the assets of the business. This function includes establishing and maintaining adequate internal control and auditing, and assuring proper insurance coverage.

This job is traditional and well understood, but it is needed to complete the picture. I have included all six of these functions in this presentation because they are needed to convey a full impression of what the controllership influence means to American business. Cost accountants have a stake and a share in this influence. It is absolutely vital, as I see it, that they understand controllership, and practice it, for controllership is a science that must be applied not alone by the controller but also by his staff and, from various points of view, by all other elements of business management as well.

THE COST CONTROL TECHNIQUE

There is a well-known phrase that joins controllers and cost accountants in an indissoluble partnership. This phrase is "cost control." It is a key technique in the successful operation of business, and it means that every controller must be a cost accountant and every cost accountant must practice controllership.

In the foregoing analysis of controllership functions, emphasis was placed very heavily on the planning and control mechanism and the controller's place in its construction and maintenance. But what about cost control, in the sense of positive, direct efforts to curb waste and actually reduce costs?

First let us admit a fundamental truth: no cost accountant or controller, acting on the privileges conferred upon him by good organization principle, has ever of himself controlled a cost or reduced a cost. This statement does not detract from the magnificent contributions which cost accountants have made to industry in the field of cost control. But this fine result must always arise from the force which he initiates and transmits to those directly responsible for incurring costs.

Every controller, like every cost accountant, is aware of the natural laws which govern his functioning—or at the very least he is being made aware of them by sharp daily experiences. He knows that his concern with cost reduction must be channeled into the organized streams of human relationship about him. He cannot give orders, cannot censure, cannot, in fact, mete out praise, because these offices are the responsibility of direct line supervision, and whenever he yields to the temptation to perform them he jeopardizes the confidence reposed in him by his operating associates.

Therefore his thinking takes a new and creative direction. He cultivates the unique talent of impelling cost reduction efforts on the part of others, and this approach is applied by the cost accountants on his staff in daily conversations with plant foremen and other supervision.

Here we find the cost accountant at his best—inspired by that attitude, rooted in controllership, which contributes most to the progress of the company—fully recognizing that his duty is properly discharged when costs are controlled by those who incur them.

THE COST CONTROL PHILOSOPHY

This philosophy is identical with that which should govern the conduct of the entire business. The quantitative basis upon which the controller's work rests is the need for a net profit. At that point he and the president are in total harmony, and from this compelling demand springs the complex accounting, standard-setting and reporting mechanism which controls the entire operation.

This demand then reaches out to its ultimate need—a plan whereby to realize the profit. It becomes the controller's mission to see that this plan is provided, in such a form that control can be exercised in relation to it. The cost accountant similarly furnishes a means for planning and control in his area of operation. The *modus operandi* is exactly the same. The plan is created by responsible management and the control exercised by the same individuals. But the idea, its power source, the educational effort that must accompany it, the procedure for its operation and the communication of operating facts which are the fuel for the machine—all emanate from the controller and his staff.

It should be evident, I think, that the success of that peculiar internal force called cost control rests on good organization and sound definition of objectives. If the controller is correctly motivated, his energy flows creatively into building a plan whereby not only costs but all other activities of the business are controlled. Cost accounting is this function as applied to a particular factory or sales operation or research assignment.

It is natural therefore that a cost accounting department should be found within the boundaries of the controller's organization. Even where the circumstances of decentralized manufacture require that a cost manager report to a factory superintendent, we almost always find that a specialized relationship called functional reporting is reserved to the controller or chief accountant at the home office. This arrangement permits an authoritative coordination of the accounting at the plant with the accounting at other locations, governed by policies centrally established. Even more important, it permits the controller to put the planning and control idea into operation throughout. Properly regulated and intelligently explained, this dual reporting scheme opens the door to effective control in a multi-plant company.

These principles of organization seem simple enough—and they are. Yet the most stubborn enemy to cost control is the failure to recognize them. In such cases the guilt seems divided between the top and line management group on the one hand and the controller and his cost accounting staff on the other. The insistence by an uninformed corporate president, for example, that the controller himself exert the control pressures and the vetoes on expenditures, that he generate cost-consciousness single handed, will invariably come to nought. So will the corresponding misconception in the minds of cost accountants and controllers, that their mission is to play the devil's advocate to every constructive proposal that involves spending money for a future return.

We must insist on a more mature attitude toward this contact point between staff control personnel and the line. It is here that the thousands of decisions are made which make product costs, and hence prices, competitive. It must become crystal clear that a continuous cost reduction effort is the responsibility of all direct line management and that controllership is to provide the means by which it is made effective.

This line of reasoning leads circuitously back to our starting point. The inference is inescapable that cost control finds its most fertile ground to be a comprehensive system of planning and control for the entire operation. Active efforts to reduce costs fall naturally within this framework, but they result from the demand for growth and profits emanating from top management and flowing directly through the line organization down to the point where the dollar is used.

PLANNING FOR CONTROL

It seems clear enough that planning precedes control. It must be equally clear how and by whom the planning is to be done. This is vital to the control process, since the mental wheels set in motion during the planning phase continue to revolve in the control phase.

Planning itself is emphatically not the responsibility of the controller. He finds a natural boundary to his activity when a procedure for planning has been established and he has provided its ignition. The plan must be established by the people who spend the money.

A factory department is a good example. Its foreman establishes its plan of operation. First, of course, he must know what is expected of him. With reference to the budgeting period adopted, he naturally asks how much he is expected to produce, on what schedule and to what quality standards. He then prepares a plan to achieve this objective. Translated into dollars, this plan becomes a budget.

Let us assume that, in the plant of which this department is a part, certain services are provided by other departments—for example, time study, methods engineering and production scheduling. The foreman then has more complex relationships to consider in his planning. He asks, in addition to the foregoing questions, by what methods and equipment he will be expected to perform his production job, how his direct labor standards will be set and in what manner the scheduling will be handled. Of course most foremen will have knowledge of these factors from previous experience. They are pertinent questions nevertheless, and proper planning demands that they be answered.

Equipped with a detailed understanding of his assignment, the foreman proceeds with the planning of personnel requirements, labor scheduling, including night shifts and lower-tier supervision, material waste expectancy, labor productivity, use of power and supplies, and all other factors entering into his area of responsibility. It is important here to note that the operational planning comes first—then the statement of the plan in the language of dollars, known as the budget.

PLANNING AND THE COST ACCOUNTANT

Skilled cost accounting counsel is a required ingredient of this budgeting. It collaborates every step of the way, and insists that the plan be constructed to satisfy the needs of control. In this effort, the cost accountant carefully preserves the staff status which is the very substance of his value to the company.

In passing, I should like here to remark about two tenets which the cost accountant must observe. First, he must establish a simple, clear system, free from technical complexities, which operating people can understand. There is no bigger obstacle to proper planning, no heavier handicap to making the foreman captain of his own destiny, than an accounting system in which the content of the accounts is obscure.

Second, no foreman should be charged for a cost over which he has no power of decision. I cannot subscribe to the theory of charging masses of overhead incurred by others up the line simply to impress the foreman that running a company is expensive. Only those items which he for the most part directly controls should find their way into his budget. The entire theory of responsibility accounting, and hence of planning and control, rests on observance of these rules.

PREDECISION AND THE MASTER PLAN

It will also be noted that constructing an operating plan requires a good deal of predecision, as to quantities, methods, labor rates and so on. Foremen not experienced in the principles of planning will say, for example: "I cannot budget labor rates for a year ahead unless you tell me whether or not we will grant another general wage increase." The question is a legitimate one, but should be put into the positive: "I will budget labor costs when you inform me whether to plan on a general wage increase and if so how much," and his factory superintendent should so inform him.

If the superintendent does not know, as is likely, then he should inquire of his superior and so on up the line. The question of labor rates to be used for company cost planning is sufficiently important to find its way to the president's office for decision. If, as is very possible, the president does not know the answer, he must specify an assumption for planning purposes so that the work may proceed. To force these decisions into being is the task of enlightened controllership.

I need not elaborate on the course followed by the departmental plan so conceived toward its destiny as a segment of the master plan guiding the entire business. If the parts fitted together do not make a profitable and satisfactory whole, they must be altered. This process, which frequently impels cost reduction, is the particular interest of controllership.

It is pertinent here to say, however, that the operating plan for the factory department which we have been considering will reach its highest value only if it becomes a segment in the whole plan for the company. This overall planning should include sales volume, manufacturing costs, all operating expenses, nonoperating items, taxes and net profit. To reach maximum effectiveness it should also include capital expenditure planning and a financial program. Such a broad base lends substance to the plan for the individual department which can be achieved in no other way.

REPORTING AND CONTROL

The final step, in the light of all the preceding reasoning, may now go under the defined term "control." Interpretive reporting is the *modus operandi*. Budget comparisons, statistical compilations, comments and reports flow constantly from the controller's staff to all levels of responsibility. Deviations from the carefully constructed plan are accented under the familiar management-by-exception principle.

The control mechanism is now complete. To use it, we focus on the points at which departures have occurred or will occur. We then find it possible either to bring the ship back to the precharted course or to alter the course. Either is acceptable, so long as it is done in the conscious knowledge of all the facts, and by decision of those responsible.

For example, the monthly budget reports reveal a cost of production in excess of budget. Because the plan has been built in detail and equipped with an orderly accounting system, it is not difficult to analyze the differences and put a finger on the cause. Having done so, we next ask: *Is this circumstance susceptible to correction or must the plan be altered to take account of the higher cost level?* The effect of the latter decision on the profit of the company must also be examined—carrying the facts to the appropriate level of responsibility.

A more typical instance of control in action is the anticipation of costs not provided in the budget. Proper planning, where the principles of control are understood and made effective, will uncover such a situation before the costs are incurred. It then becomes possible to get advance approval for exceeding budget, if such action seems desirable. It must here be remembered that the budget is a guide rather than a ceiling—that it furnishes the means for considering intelligently those expenditures which will transcend its limits.

It is nowhere clearer than at this point in the management process that effective planning and control rests on principles of sound organization. Delegation of responsibility, definition of function, the basic relationship of line and staff, all should have been clarified and applied before attempting the use of planning and control in its modern sense.

Control then must be seen as a refined process of management thought, exercised directly but made possible through indirect application by men trained in and attuned to a high calibre of staff work. Not all men are suited for this discipline of thought and purpose. Cost accountants are especially qualified to make the effort. The challenge is offered to them and to controllers alike to rise higher in the quality of service they give. Industry is hungry for this contribution. The future of planning and control as an essential of business operation seems unlimited if its practitioners are willing to devote their best efforts to it.

BUDGETS: PRINCIPLES OF HUMAN RELATIONSHIPS

THE BUDGET COMES OF AGE †

by

James L. Peirce

ANY technique of management reaches maturity when, after its earlier mistakes have antagonized human beings sufficiently, it emerges with a new outlook and practice that is in harmony with the basic motivations of people. Budgeting now seems to be undergoing this metamorphosis. Out of the disturbance it has created is appearing a calmer, more orderly, more positive approach.

It is my purpose in this article to add weight to the spreading view that budgeting rests on principles which have more in common with concepts of human relationship than with rules of accounting; and that, if these principles are applied, successful practice is inevitable.

DEFENSIVENESS—THE TROUBLE

There is no doubt that thousands of management people are well grounded in constructive budget practice and derive from it a sense of balance and direction in their business affairs. No businessman who has had extensive experience with an ably managed budget system appears to doubt its value. But there are many more thousands who are so confused on the subject that it might indeed be better for them to discard their budgets entirely than to continue as they are. Surveys have shown that in some quarters budgeting is about as popular among foremen as a layoff, and analyses stress the damage that results from the misuse of budgeting procedures.

Some executives freely admit the shortcomings of their budget practices and acknowledge that they could be remedied by the application of more intelligent human relations. If it is as simple as that, then why cannot budgets be made a welcome and productive feature of all business operation without delay? The answer, I think, is that the problem is not such a simple one—just as human beings are not simple, just as the science of human

†This article is based on a talk presented at the Financial Management Conference of the American Management Association, New York, November 20, 1953. Reprinted from the *Harvard Business Review*, May-June 1954, pp. 58-66, copyright 1954, with permission of Harvard Business School Publishing. Similar articles were published under the title "Budgets and People: A Positive Approach," in *Guides to Modern Financial Planning*, Financial Management Series Number 104 (New York: American Management Association, 1953), pp. 3-13, and under the title "A Positive Approach to Budgets and People," in *The Financial Manager's Job* (New York: American Management Association, 1964), pp. 180-192.

relationships is not simple, as witness the many failures to apply it effectively.

How shall we go about the task of instilling revitalized ideas in place of negative or short-sighted attitudes?

We can accomplish nothing until we face up to the fact that many of us have acquired a defensive approach to the subject through painful experience. Here we must dig deep into the recesses of thought—not omitting the realm of emotional misconception that colors our word associations. Why do the two words "budgets" and "people" repel each other? Why should they, when taken together, suggest the image of a problem? Why, in fact, should it even be necessary to discuss a positive approach to the matter of budgets and people?

This unhappy reaction comes from the fact that people generally do not like budgets. We must remember that foremen are people first and supervisors second; so are department managers and top executives. Budgets represent restriction. They are in the same category as school bells and Monday mornings. Each of us has entered business life with a primitive aversion to restraint, only thinly veneered by academic training.

Someone should have presented the budget idea to us very constructively in order for us to accept it, much less to enjoy it. If from the very beginning of our careers we had been told, with accompanying evidence, that budgets were a help to us, affording us guidance, stability, and strength, as well as keeping us out of innumerable troubles, our responses would by now be quite different.

But what was our actual experience? Have not many of us been introduced to budgets in business when the budget was blamed, rightly or wrongly, for our failure to get a raise in pay? Have not many of us become acquainted with the budget only as a barrier to spending what we felt were necessary amounts of money for better equipment or performance? Is it surprising, then, that budgets are associated in many people's minds with paucity and niggardliness rather than with planning and direction?

Fortunately, it is not too late to effect a correction in the thinking of the current generation of managers.

ATTITUDES—THE KEY

In probing further, it quickly becomes evident that good attitudes are the key to successful budgeting. When the attitudes of people toward each other are generous, understanding, and based on mutual respect, any technique adopted by management to further effective performance is apt to be successful. When human attitudes are dominated by distrust, criticism, and recrimination, any technique designed to improve performance is likely to fail miserably. In such cases, by a strange twist of human nature, the budgets and those who defend them bear the brunt of the blame for more fundamental errors which are entirely unconnected with budgets.

Budgeting is a trained, disciplined approach to all problems, which recognizes the need for standards of performance in order to achieve a result. Hence it must be built on a base of good organization; otherwise, favorable attitudes have no chance to operate. But at the same time it lives in an atmosphere of perpetual adjustment to the needs and capacities of people. It thrives on such fundamentals as recognition of accomplishment, consideration for the rights of individuals, fair play—in other words, enlightened relationships among people.

Motivation for Budgeting

In exploring budgeting principles as they relate to people, the first consideration should be the motivation for the budget system. Why have one at all? Is the budget a part of a system of overall planning, in order that all concerned may have a measure of the amounts to be spent, and in order that action may be by design rather than by expediency? Or is the budget a pressure device designed to goad people into greater efforts? It takes a little soul-searching to determine honestly which of these concepts represents the position of a particular management.

Both concepts are prevalent. They may be symbolized by two wooden sticks—one neatly divided into thirty-six one-inch spaces, and the other sharply pointed at one end. The yardstick, symbolizing the planning concept of budgets, may be used, for example, by a foreman to establish standards of performance and cost and to measure actual results in relation thereto; in this sense, it is a tool used by the foreman and his boss in partnership. The pointed stick, a symbol of the pressure type of budget, is always found in the hand of the superior, turned menacingly toward his foremen or workers. The yardstick concept elicits the voluntary effort of men to do their best work. The pointed stick forces a reluctant and minimal performance.

There is plenty of evidence that the choice of the yardstick concept will not diminish the yield from the budget tool in terms of cost reduction. It has been shown again and again that high costs which stubbornly resist all efforts of the pressure type will melt away under the warmth of an approach which is attuned to the basic responses of humanity. The attitude to be adopted here is an enlistment of all concerned in a common effort, with a complete explanation of objectives and methods.

PLANNING—THE FOUNDATION

Next in line of exploration of principles is the dependence of budgets on general company planning. Although budgeting can be separately applied to any unit of the business, it is far more effective when it rests on a foundation of integrated planning for the entire operation. In the proper sense, it is only one phase of planning. When the planning concept has been adopted, budgets emerge of necessity—budgets with a purpose as deep as the stream of ideas giving direction and drive to the business itself.

The presence or absence of intelligent planning is reflected to a surprising degree in the effectiveness of the people who are asked to operate with a budget system. And this means all the people—from top executives to production-line workers. Individuals are usually more intuitive than we realize. When a budget is built on sound business planning, they respond to that fact without always knowing why.

Meaning of Planning

As used in this discussion, *planning* refers to the predetermination of a course of action in such detail that every responsible unit of the company may be guided thereby. It includes sales forecasting, production scheduling, expense budgeting, and estimating of manufacturing costs and inventory levels. It involves making advance decisions concerning new product development and introduction, merchandising methods, material procurement, and labor rates. In short, planning implies anticipating all the knotty problems to be met by a business during the planning period—usually a year so far as operations are concerned, longer for financial and developmental activities—in other words, facing the problems and making decisions about them *ahead of time*, (subject to later revision if necessary).

These decisions are frequently so hard to make in advance that they border on the impossible. Yet they insure a reasonable net profit as no other method can. And on this planned net profit figure—the apex of the planning structure—depends our ability to attract new capital as needed and to compensate management and shareholders.

I need not elaborate the importance of profit planning. I am only concerned here that it be recognized that when budgeting has a hard core of deliberate planning, adhered to by the company's top, middle, and all other management, the budget idea takes on real meaning for all concerned. Without this basis, it can never be completely palatable to those who do not understand how it can benefit them.

Effect on People

Let us examine the effect of the planning process on the people involved in it. In particular, we might first consider the impact on administrative people, for their outlook in the long run determines the attitudes of the larger nonadministrative group. What is the planning technique doing to the foremen, department managers, division heads? Is it building up or tearing down their confidence in their company's future? Is it affecting favorably or adversely their independence of thought, their self-assurance, their capacity to understand and rely on those around them?

It seems self-evident that planning alone does not afford the entire answer. If a company's administrative personnel are exhibiting what is called "good morale" before the installation of a planning system, the chances are that turning their eyes to the future and asking them to construct together a plan for better achievement can do them no harm, but can do them untold good. With proper explanations, the management can hold forth the legitimate promise of better accomplishment, greater satisfaction, more confident operating, and, ultimately, opportunity for increased compensation.

If, on the other hand, the management is struggling with a discordant staff, perhaps suffering from the blight of fuzzy organization lines or any of the other impediments to good work resulting from a mediocre job of personnel administration, it might be better off to defer trying the planning and control idea until it has put its house in order. Too frequently a well-designed budget system has collapsed after being superimposed on a faulty base of administrative personnel policy. Then the budget is discarded and all concerned return to their familiar bad habits.

CONTROL—THE COMPLEMENT

But there is another phase of budgeting which tests the fiber of men even more than planning. I am referring to control, which is the eternal complement of planning. Neither one is useful without the other, and to budget even the smallest units of a business implies the presence of control also.

Budget Abuses

It is in the control area that the colossal mistakes of budgeting are made. It is here that the amateurs have censured their subordinates for exceeding budgets, without realizing that they themselves were to blame for inadequate training. It is here that men have become so frustrated under maladministered budgets that they have resorted to all sorts of tricks to conceal the actual results and have padded their budgets to give themselves breathing room. It is here that staff men have usurped authority, merited pay increases have been denied because of budget limitations, and tales have been carried around supervision and up to the top under the guise of budget reporting.

The list of abuses could be prolonged indefinitely. There are many wrong ways to exercise budget control. There is only one right way. Let us then discard the negative approach, since the assertion of an affirmative truth will dissolve all counterfeits.

Control might be quickly and simply defined as a disciplined effort to follow a plan or explain deviations from it. The effort referred to takes the form of self-discipline—voluntary, unified, and cooperative. The deviations from plan are deliberate, foreknown, and authorized. If they are apparently beyond anyone's ability to prevent—as for instance a failure to reach budgeted sales volume—at least they are spotlighted as early as possible, and management has the chance to take whatever action is indicated. Control is simply the modern form of the old formula, "management by exception."

It is, of course, at the point of deviation from the budget that most of the human problems are born. This is, by design, the central point in the entire system—the moment which demands explanation, instruction, decision, argument, or even discipline, as the case warrants—the flash point for management in action.

Common-Sense Departures

It should be evident that the effect of control on people is commensurate with their training and conditioning for it. If they understand thoroughly the meaning and uses of control, they will view it in the light of common sense. They will neither resent it nor be awed by it. They will turn it to the constructive use for which it is intended, and it will become an aid rather than an obstacle.

Perhaps the best way to clarify this common-sense approach is to examine a typical situation in which a manager wishes to make what he believes to be a desirable expenditure not covered in his budget. This problem is encountered daily and solved without friction by management people equipped with knowledge of budget principles and skill in their application—in other words, by the trained minority which shows the same attitudes-in-action of a manager grounded in good budget practice as illustrated in the following case:

The case of a sales promotion manager who is also responsible for advertising—Having been instructed to prepare a budget, he has first carefully completed his sales promotion and advertising plans for the coming period, basing them on discussions with the sales vice president and others responsible for policy and sales objectives. After constructing an acceptable plan, he has converted it into dollars in the form of a budget, which has been approved.

Because he has prepared this budget himself, he is thoroughly familiar with it. It is supported with adequate detail, including schedules of space insertions, estimates of costs of mailings, salary lists, and so on. He has reached an understanding with his "boss" concerning all of these items as a preliminary to approval of the budget. He feels confident that the plan and budget are as nearly right as he can make them.

Furthermore, he knows the implications of accepting this budget as his guide to operations. It is not to be exceeded without approval. It is a commitment that must be honored, and he well understands its importance to the company, his associates, and himself.

Nevertheless, he senses in the attitudes surrounding his budget an element of flexibility. If conditions change, the budget will have to be altered, either upward or downward. The sales promotion manager is not uneasy about this prospect. He is simply alert to recognize such a situation if it should develop.

Now let us suppose that an opportunity is presented to exert extra pressure on a certain market, and it appears that a special direct-mail campaign, supplemented by some local newspaper advertising, will yield good sales results. He knows enough not to throw the whole idea aside simply because it is not provided for in his budget. He has already had a clear understanding with the top sales executive about what to do in such cases. So he goes about preparing a report, including proposed action, cost, and anticipated results; and he presents this report, knowing that it will be given proper consideration, even though it represents an expenditure in excess of budget limits.

The important point here is that this man, as manager of sales promotion, will not be subjected to injustice, censure, or negative treatment of any sort in advancing his ideas. He is fully aware of having a plan and a commitment to abide by it; yet he has assurance that if the interests of the company will be best served by breaking the budget, permission to do so will be forthcoming. All concerned will have an opportunity to evaluate the proposal and to weigh the desirability of deviating from the adopted plan.

How simple this miniature study in budget attitudes! How mature the responses governed by common sense! And yet how often common sense is violated! Is there any reason not to extend this frank approach to the foreman who sees a need for maintenance expenses or a merit increase not embraced in his budget? The frictions, frustrations, and other evils supposed to be inherent in budgets must all be susceptible to eradication in the same sensible manner.

Essential Prerequisites

All this presupposes, of course, that the supervisor in question—regardless of which division of the business he may be in—enjoys a satisfactory working relationship with his immediate superior. It also rests on clear-cut organization lines and the disposition to delegate authority along with responsibility.

Further, the accounting principles used must be well tested, and the accounting administration of high caliber. Strict honesty must govern the determination of the content of budget accounts and of the charges made thereto. Nothing confuses budget operation more quickly than the charging of costs over which the supervisor has no control, unless such items are set out separately and so labeled.

A last important requisite is understanding the make-up of the budget. Flexible factory budgets especially can be complicated and subject to dispute. The factors used must be clearly explained, with full recognition of their weaknesses. If an item—such as machine repairs, for example—is neither wholly fixed nor wholly variable, but must be treated one way or the other for budget purposes, the shortcomings of the resulting budget figure should be conceded frankly. If scrap and rework costs are subject to dispute between foremen, the situation must be talked out in an air of give-and-take.

No plant management should encourage or permit embittered arguments between foremen on such a matter. If all concerned have a clear understanding of the function of the budget and a reasonable attitude toward each other in the framework of modern industrial organization, such disputes will not occur.

COST REDUCTION—THE GOAL

The attitudes we have been discussing should add to, rather than detract from, the effectiveness of budgets in the field of cost control. Most companies operate continuously, in good times and bad, under the pressure of relentless competition, which forces them in turn to devote ceaseless effort to cost reduction. It is perhaps this circumstance more than any other that has given impetus to the spread of budgeting. And it has doubtless given rise to the abuses falling under the general heading of "pressure."

The usual tone of the complaints in this category is to the effect that budgets are used only as a hammer on costs (and at the same time on people), and particularly that the budgets are constantly being tightened and compliance with them enforced indiscriminately. The impression received by a supervisor in this situation is one of constant insistence on better and better performance, continuous blame for failure to meet the budget, and complete absence of credit for his good work. The budget becomes purely a pressure device against which he must defend himself or lose his job.

The only really effective cure for such a distorted outlook is to substitute, as rapidly as possible, a "let's do it together" attitude for the shortsighted "you do it or else" attitude. The latter may have gained more ground in a plant or office than the management realizes. To correct this attitude may take time and patience, but it is never impossible to blank out negatives and substitute positives in human thinking.

Cost reduction drive is a feature of the American competitive system and is admittedly responsible in large measure for our high living standard. Budgets can be used for such stimulation without enslaving people. They furnish the standard from which to explore cost-savings possibilities. They provide the measure of yield from improved methods. But the attitude surrounding the practice must be right.

Incentives, True and False

This line of thought runs directly into the question of incentive. What incentive does a production supervisor have to reduce costs? Certainly the incentive supplied by threat is negative and, in the long run, ineffective. Direct money incentives, correlated to budget factors, claim some merit but, as we shall see, are fraught with problems. The true incentives, becoming clear after generations of management experiment, are those usually referred to as "intangible," supplemented by wages carefully determined and sympathetically explained.

But as an alternative let us examine for a moment the possibilities of direct money incentives. Some companies use and defend them—and we can have no quarrel with success. The line of reasoning on which they are based runs something like this: "If simple piecework can be an effective incentive for the workman, then the same principle can be applied to the foreman. We will provide a supervisory bonus and include in its computation a factor measuring success in complying with the budget. Savings against the budget will benefit the company and, at the same time, will provide funds for rewarding the foreman."

The fallacies in this reasoning begin to appear early in the process. They arise from two sources: (a) from the almost insurmountable difficulty of setting a completely fair and acceptable budget for this purpose, especially in the light of unforeseeable changes in operating conditions, and (b) from the tendency for the foreman to emphasize budget performance to the detriment of necessary action. It is a distinct temptation to defer maintenance when the need is not urgent and the expenditure would reduce one's own paycheck.

As the foreman grows to the stature of a responsible manager, as he becomes, more and more able to carry added responsibilities independently (and this is the goal of enlightened management today), the problems of basing incentive pay on budget factors become progressively tougher to handle. The experienced foreman is conscious of the importance of cost reduction, both by training and by virtue of the understanding of the job which his company has given him. He is also conscious of the need to spend money. He is likely to resent being rewarded for unwise penny-pinching as much as being penalized for exceeding his budget when the need for it is evident to everyone.

To a supervisor properly informed and aware of his role as a part of the management team, the real incentive is the satisfaction that comes from knowing that he has given his best effort, evidenced by suitable recognition both financial and in the manner and words of the superior. There is no substitute for the positive kind of understanding that can be developed between a supervisor and the rest of management if all concerned resolve to cultivate it.

By the same token, there is nothing better to assure the success of a cost-reduction program than a foreman with an inspired attitude and a real comprehension of the company's objectives, needs, and policies. To such a man, the budget will be a tool used to measure common achievements, rather than an irritant to the men and women entrusted to his leadership.

MANAGEMENT SUPPORT—THE NEED

One of the rocks on which many systems founder is the lack of top-management support. This is a strange commentary on a management group which, in this country, is generally supposed to have reached the acme of sophistication in the motivation of people. Nevertheless, examine any limping, halfhearted budget system, and note how the "chickens come home to roost" in the president's office.

Even more surprising, it frequently turns out that the top man does not really understand the planning and control concept and the simple interplay of attitudes that make it work. Consequently his allegiance to it is tentative and lukewarm. He constantly questions the methods used and is instinctively distrustful of results. This frame of mind permeates the organization. It bolsters opposition to the budget idea and weakens its proponents.

No budget system can realize its potential value without the unqualified support and understanding of top management. The solution, of course, lies in a process usually known as "education." Actually, it is even deeper than that. The budget idea is an expanding, growing concept—usually pioneered by one man with vision in a company. Little by little, this man—be he president or controller—patiently inculcates the advancing idea on his associates, until it is tested and accepted by all.

Controllers' Mistakes

There is another enemy of successful budget practice which may well be the cause of more of the friction between budgets and people than all the other errors put together. I refer to the misconception on the part of controllers, budget managers, accountants, and other staff people concerning their part in the process.

When a controller takes operating personnel to task for exceeding the budget, he is inviting trouble of the worst kind. His correct course is to report the situation to responsible operating management and, if necessary, to the president, using the same figures and terms in each case. The problem then rests with the president and his operating subordinate, which is exactly where it belongs. It should be discussed and action determined in the direct line organization. No controller should permit himself to be placed in the position of representing the president in such matters of giving approval to budgets or disapproval to results.

The same principle applies to all staff people concerned with coordinating the budget system, whether they report to a controller, treasurer, or factory accountant. There is impressive evidence that overzealous budget people have caused a great deal of mischief in this field, practically all of it unnecessary. They cannot be blamed individually, of course, for the failure of management to provide the principles needed for good budget practice. The remedy is in the eradication of a vicious set of faulty notions concerning the relationships of staff and line.

One of the first steps is to insist that each manager or foreman establish his own budget. He knows best his potential performance and the extent to which he can commit himself. He may enlist expert help of course, from the budget man, but under no circumstances should the budget man or controller establish the budget, nor should the foreman be permitted to feel that this is happening. The penalty for violating this rule is the sacrifice of the sense of responsibility that locks a man securely to his budget when he knows it is his own.

Another misconception sometimes indulged by budget men is that they are almost solely responsible for cost reduction; that they alone are expected to seek and find opportunities for cost savings, such as excessive waste, dispensable overtime, carelessness in handling tools, and so on. In some cases, they have apparently been instructed to report such instances to a factory superintendent or even to top management rather than to the responsible first-line supervisor. It is difficult to conceive of a practice that violates more completely the basic principles of good human relations.

Line Organization

This medieval mess will clear itself up once management has established the fact that the line organization is responsible for cost control—fully and absolutely. Using a familiar type of organization, let it be clear that the vice president of manufacturing is charged with the duty of conducting the manufacturing cost reduction campaign; he delegates this work as he sees fit to plant managers, and they in turn to factory superintendents, who then look to the front-line men, the foremen, for control of costs.

The controller and budget men still fit into this picture importantly:

    (1) They are equipped to establish and coordinate the budget system, with all of the tools of accounting and cost analysis.

    (2) They should be able to teach the operating people how to use it.

    (3) They should provide timely and intelligible reporting on performance against budget. (This reporting should of course be tailored to the organization level to which it is addressed. For instance, at the top, the controller is obligated to report that which is pertinent to the president of the company.)

The attitude which should govern the staff people in this field, as in all other staff assignments, is one of maximum helpfulness to the line personnel. Only in this way can the budget man gain the foreman's confidence. If he finds cost-saving ideas, they should be volunteered promptly to the foreman for what use the latter can make of them. Personal credit is not the primary consideration. The budget man's own superior should be adept enough in detecting a skillful job to accord it the recognition it deserves—and one primary evidence of such performance will be a satisfactory relationship with the operating personnel. It is a preposterous notion that a budget man vaults to success on the failures and errors of the line.

CONCLUSION

The specific steps to be taken to improve budgeting practice depend, of course, on the mistakes an organization has been making. A searching self-examination in the light of the known principles of budgeting would seem to be the first move. Having identified the practices in an organization which most clearly abuse these principles, management will find that the corrective steps will present themselves. Courage and patience are needed to follow them.

Summary of Principles

Here, for your convenience, is a summary of points to be considered by any management wishing to establish its budget practice on a sound foundation:

(1) Establish your budget system on the highest possible level of motivation. To be specific, this means using it as a means for setting standards of performance, for measuring actual results, and for guiding management to satisfactory achievement. It means rejecting the use of budgets primarily as a pressure device to goad people into greater efforts. Accept this as a part of the philosophy of your company. Think about it, talk about it, make it a reality. And give more than lip service, even if it is difficult at first to separate the two conflicting motives. A budget program cannot be advanced to the stage of maximum fruition without this step.

(2) Anchor your budgeting firmly in a foundation of company planning. Do not permit it to float unattached—a technique without a clearly thought-out reason for being. The budget is not the plan; it is merely the statement of the plan in the language of figures. First turn the thinking of your organization to basic planning; then ask your people to prepare budgets to effectuate their plans. Plan sales by markets and products, plan development, plan methods of manufacturing, purchasing, and merchandising. Determine the performance required of each department of the business; then budgets become simply the standard of dollars needed to do the job. This is the approach that makes managers out of men.

(3) Establish the meaning of control, and then put it into practice. In particular this requires the manager of each department to establish his own budget, based on his understanding of the job to be done. Top management may not be able to approve as high a figure as he asks for, but it can reach agreement with him as to what he is expected to accomplish and what it will cost. Having done this, he is responsible for planned performance. If he finds it necessary to exceed the budget, he should discuss this action with his superior and ask for advance approval. A budget is neither to be considered sacred nor to be taken lightly. Managers will respond with better attitudes when they understand that the use of the budget is to permit them to control their own operations.

84

(4)   Insist on a clear-cut organization structure. A budget system cannot thrive without it. Each department should have a responsible manager, vested with authority commensurate with his responsibilities. He should have a clear understanding both as to the individual to whom he reports and as to the people who report to him. These are well-known precepts. A searching organization audit may be needed to determine whether they are being followed. The limitations on budget success are precisely marked by the degree of organization soundness.

(5)   Arrange for good, common-sense accounting and complete, simple, and prompt explanations of the content of the items. This requires an accounting staff that is more concerned with the operating facts than with the techniques of balancing the books. Extreme care should be devoted to seeing that no supervisor has in his budget any item over which he does not have control. This area is fraught with debatable items and unending technical complications. If your house is not in order in this respect, almost any amount of effort is justified to put it in shape. And unless you are the exception to the rule, it will cost more money initially than you expect to pay, in terms of staff salaries and, perhaps, outside consulting services. The cost is usually well justified, however, in the end result.

(6)   In the field of cost control, use your budget as a tool to be placed in your foremen's hands—not as a club to be held over their heads. To implement this rule, it may be a good idea to design an educational program. Meetings attended by line and staff supervisors may prove an effective vehicle. Cost reduction must be placed on the basis of mutual effort toward a common aim. The creation of this atmosphere is an essential, definitive step in budget practice.

(7)   Insure the active participation of top management. The budget program cannot succeed otherwise. The way of going about this step depends on your organizational status. If you are the president and question how well you measure up to this requirement, examine your thinking critically and ascertain which of the points in this article, if any, arouse resistance in your thought. Discussion with a controller other than your own may afford a fresh view. In any case, set aside the time to explore and understand the subject fully and to practice budgetary control in your daily affairs. If, however, you are a controller, your course in enlisting top-management support is one of patient, untiring teaching, until your case is won and the planning and control idea is in the warp and wool of your company's thinking.

(8)   See that the controller and his staff express the correct attitude for the responsibility they undertake with respect to budgets. It is the controller's job to establish, maintain, and coordinate a budgetary system—in fact, a complete system of planning and control. But this work must be accomplished through authorized management. He must not enforce his instructors nor issue orders. He and his staff must be devoted to producing, reporting, and interpreting information—to making the planning and control machinery run. He is wholly a staff executive, and his only honors stem from the confidence of his associates. This he earns by honestly providing the control service and refraining from making operating decisions. Perhaps the cultivation of this attitude is the most productive single step of all, because from it the impetus to take the other steps may flow.

I have refrained from specifying the manner in which these ideas might be made known, or "sold," to the administrative groups. The task is essentially one for controllership. It is the most challenging project the controller is privileged to conduct, and it gains momentum as he enlists the support of top management and of supervision at all levels.

The actual method of carrying on this unremitting campaign varies from company to company, but there is a predominant tendency to rely largely on daily contacts. The controller and his staff—all the budget men and cost accountants—spread the idea in their working conversations. Meanwhile, special attention is continuously given the top echelon by the controller himself. Relatively few companies appear to hold regular educational or discussion meetings for this purpose.

It is interesting that all of the eight steps listed have their roots deep in personnel administration—that each one is, in the final analysis, the reflection of a problem involving people.

Deeper Significance

The present era demands a new appraisal of our daily work. The symptoms of budget irritations may point to deeper meanings in the spiritual emancipation of mankind. We are beginning to learn that no tool can be used effectively unless the hand that guides it is rightly motivated. Like all other techniques of business, the budget should be a door open to more satisfying and profitable work—not an instrument of torture.

Then it will be known that what you can do without a budget you can do better with one. It will be seen that the entire planning and control procedure, under whatever name, is a device for freeing men to do their best work—not a machine of restriction and condemnation. This better view is within our grasp today.

Planning is but another word for the vision that sees a creative achievement before it is manifest. Control is but a name for direction. The genius of management cannot fail to turn the budget idea finally into positive channels, so that people individually, as well as business leadership generally, will reap the harvest that it promises.

WHAT MAKES A BUDGET WORK? †
by
James L. Peirce

ABOUT the only thing I can offer you as an excuse for my being here tonight is my own experience. There is certainly nothing new to be said about the principles of budgeting. Business and management periodicals are replete with ideas of all sorts on the subject, hundreds of books have been written on it, and hundreds of thousands of words of intracompany conversation have been devoted to the never ending questions it raises.

Still, strange as it seems, the field of budgeting is still alive, and people still ask each other about their experiences in it. I think there is a reason for this. I think it is because we are just beginning to see it all in a new light. The door has just opened a crack to reveal the grandeur of a new viewpoint—that budgeting is not figures, standards and mathematics, but, rather, it is people. It is people's thoughts, people's attitudes, even the emotions of people that make or break a budgeting program.

When these ideas and attitudes are skillfully cultivated and channeled, and when we have at the same time a management honestly motivated and sincere in its efforts, the budget can be made to work.

Now that these facts are becoming more clearly recognized, more and more companies are enabled to look backward a few years and see their own mistakes, standing out like fence posts. By so doing they may be able to turn them into guideposts, so that other companies may profit thereby. It is with this hope that I undertake to give you tonight a short review of our experience with budgeting principles.

As we go along, I am sure you will understand what I mean when I say there is not an original thought in anything I am going to tell you. Nor does it rest on anything mysterious or abstruse. The principles of budgeting are simple. When they are intuitively practiced by everyone, we will no longer need to spend our evenings discussing them.

Furthermore, these ideas, you will find to be largely the reflection of your own thinking. We all tend, in any field of science, to follow our individual mental channels to identical fundamental conclusions. This is illustrated in the parallelism in developments in military science on both sides of the iron curtain—a phenomenon far too persistent to be accounted for by coincidence or by treason among a few researchers.

†Talk delivered before the Illinois Manufacturers' Costs Association, January 18, 1955. Reprinted from the *Illinois Manufacturers' Costs Association Monthly Bulletin*, April 1955, 6 printed pages, with permission of the Illinois Manufacturers' Association.

All I can really hope to do, then, is to restate some of the things we know in a way that will either confirm your convictions if you have already reached the same results, or agitate your thinking if you have not.

BUDGETING IS A SCIENCE

The fascinating thing about budgeting is that it is a science—and, like any science, it can be practiced according to fixed principles and rules. If these are followed, the budget practice is successful; if they are not, the budget practice is proportionately unsuccessful.

Well then, why do we not—all of us—pay more attention to the task of uncovering, developing, stating and disseminating these rules and principles? If we do not, our businesses will be outdone by the companies which do; and we will be victims of competition, not in products or markets, but in progressive management.

Not only is budgeting a science, but as a science, it has unique characteristics which are seldom acknowledged. As I have already hinted, it is a science of human relationships rather than figures. It is positively grounded in suck things as individual incentives, personnel development, sound organization principles and human values. Properly handled, it establishes mutual goals, cooperative efforts to achieve them, and the wholesome atmosphere of free enterprise within the many little business units which we call departments.

To make of ourselves an effective case history, I will have to ask your indulgence if I give you a brief portrait of our company. We have been manufacturers of office duplicating equipment and supplies for some seventy years. Nearly all of our plant facilities and our general offices are under one roof in suburban Chicago, comprising about 600,000 feet of floor space. We have about 1,700 employees. Our production is divided between duplicating machines, which is mechanical fabrication and assembly, and duplicating supplies, which is chemical and paper processing.

The products are thought of in the trade as a specialty line and do not lend themselves to mass production methods. They are marketed through about 240 independent distributors in the United States and to a small extent in foreign countries. We also do some business in sub-assemblies classifiable as munitions.

CASE HISTORY

We took our first faltering steps in the budgeting field in the late thirties, when we began to prepare budgets for various general office and plant departments, and for the twenty retail branches which we maintained at that time. The idea germinated in the office of the Controller (my predecessor) and from there burst like a Fourth of July bombshell over the rest of the organization.

It took quite a long time to convince the management of that day—seasoned and steeped in the more autocratic methods of an earlier era—that budgets were needed at all. By the nature of things, someone had to act, and the Controller therefore established the expense budgets. He then informed the various department managers as to the amount of each item therein, at the same time getting the approval of the president.

Perhaps you can visualize, or have yourselves experienced, the friction produced by this setup. No one was quite certain who was responsible for enforcement. The budgets were accepted in various ways by the individual managers—with enthusiasm, with tolerance, or under protest. All were somewhat confused, but the show was on the road, at least, and though the Controller's popularity ebbed to a new low, we had the beginnings of a budget system.

Out of this confusion came our first big, valuable lesson. It was costly in both money and time, but worth every dollar and every hour of its costs. The lesson seems elementary to us all now, yet every so often we hear of its being ignored. It is simple this: that a man must make his own budget. If a given department manager is to be held accountable to a budget, he himself must be permitted to establish that budget.

CAN A DEPARTMENT SET ITS OWN BUDGET?

To put it another way, you hire a man to do a specific job—and I don't care whether the job is to run a screw machine department or to merchandise umbrellas in Brazil—and the first thing you do is to define carefully the job you want done. With that part understood, you then ask him what he will have to spend in order to accomplish it. He tells you and if you approve his requirements, that becomes his budget.

If you do not approve, then you discuss the matter with him, and perhaps you get him to agree to a different plan. The important thing is that, as a responsible manager and an independent thinking individual, not dominated nor intimidated by you or anyone else, he agrees to the dollar amount. It becomes his own and he accepts it in a responsible way. Knowing the job to be done, he has established his budget. No one can successfully do it for him.

While we are on this point, let us take a moment to dispel the specious counter-argument—that when you allow a man to set his own budget, you have lost control. In the first place—assuming you are his boss—you have defined the job he is to do and you retain the right to direct his activities. You appraise his results and you are the principal factor in his compensation and promotion. Exercised wisely, these prerogatives ought to be more than enough to keep you man from going off the beam in establishing his budget.

Furthermore, we came upon another interesting truth in the early days of our budget adventuring. Strange though it seemed at that time, men set their own budgets too low oftener than they set them too high.

This arose from various causes. Partly it was ignorance, by which I mean the tendency to omit provision for any unforseen contingencies whatever, ignoring the lessons of the past. Partly it was overoptimism. Partly it reflected the confident anticipation of doing a good job and the wholesome willingness to work to a tight standard. Generally speaking, the practice of padding budgets did not appear until we had made a second major mistake, namely adhering rigidly to a budget figure despite changes in conditions for which the man could not be held responsible.

WHEN SHALL THE BUDGET BE ADJUSTED?

This leads to lesson number two, drawn directly from experience. We had to learn the hard way that there are circumstances in which the budget must be exceeded without adverse effect on the appraisal of performance.

Conditions surrounding a given operation simply will not remain static. They change, and the light in which yesterday's decisions were made is not the light of today. New demands are levied, new contingencies encountered, new challenges faced. Spending more than the amount budgeted may well be in the best interest of the company.

For example, when new or improved products reach the end of their long course, which has taken them from the idea stage through research, development, design, prototype, testing, redesign, tooling, and so on, they are at last ready for introduction to the field. It is at this moment that sales promotion and advertising effort must be applied. If this acceleration of the expense level has not been provided in the budget, something must be done to permit the expenditure, in order not to lose the value of proper timing in putting the item into the market.

Now if good planning underlies the preparation of budgets, this particular type of incident will be relatively rare. Nevertheless similar situations will always persist in business. Good common sense will dictate going over budget limitations.

How shall this be accomplished without wrecking the foundations of the budget structure? It is certain that the way *not* to do it is to encourage the responsible manager to go ahead and spend the money, unsure whether or not his action will be approved, afterward, with a guilt complex, to beard a frowning controller.

Another of the more popular wrong methods is to refuse to spend the money because it is not provided in the budget, even at the risk of injury to the company. One of the waymarks in our budget progress occurred in this area. A foreman, when asked for a raise by one of his men, admitted that the man was entitled to it, but refused to grant it on the ground that it was not provided in his budget. In the ensuing crisis, we were forced to undergo what a [John Foster] Dulles might have called an "agonizing reappraisal" of our budget attitudes, and particularly of the understanding of those attitudes in our supervisory organization.

Perhaps it is now time to look at the *right* method of exceeding budget. Having learned the lesson, we find that this circumstance occurs regularly and without undue friction. As an illustration, let us assume an unforeseen delay in the design of a new machine, requiring several weeks more time than anticipated to produce the parts drawings. Faced with this situation, the Manufacturing Division realizes at once that its Tool Room cannot turn out the required tools to produce the model in time for the scheduled introduction date.

The alternative to failure to introduce the item to the field on time is to farm out some of the fabrication of tools to an outside shop, at a cost well in excess of producing them internally. This course of action will have several effects on the company's budgets. The increase in cost of the tools known as perishable (those not capitalized) will represent a breach of the Master Mechanic's expense budget for several months. The increase in cost of the tools known as permanent (those capitalized and amortized) will cause an excess over the Master Mechanic's capital expenditure budget. The amortization charge for the higher cost of tools will also be greater than planned, thereby raising charges to current operations after the tools have been put into use.

The Master Mechanic, who is responsible for the Tool Room, estimates the amount by which it will be necessary to exceed these budgets, and explains the matter to the Vice President-Manufacturing.

The latter in turn explains it to the President, who is the executive responsible for the company's profits. Perhaps the President then consults with the Vice President-Sales, who informs him that delay in the date of introduction of the machine will seriously damage the morale of the distributing organization, because they have been told of the forthcoming new model. Conferences may follow with the Vice President-Research and Engineering, who makes it clear that acceleration of parts design cannot be effected in his division.

Fur may fly and temperatures rise as ways are sought to compensate for the failure of planning or performance, as the case may be. Let us assume in this instance, however, that the President reaches a decision to authorize the Manufacturing Division to exceed its budget by arranging with an outside tool shop to produce a portion of the tools required to put the item into production on schedule. The decision is transmitted to the Vice President-Manufacturing and thence to the Master Mechanic, who proceeds to carry it out. He exceeds his budget with full confidence that he is not only authorized to do so by his boss, but that his action fits into the framework of the budget control system. He also is aware that it has had proper consideration by all concerned and that it is in the best interest of the company.

It seems to me that you may well have here the difference between a confident, effective manager and one who is unsure of himself because he is hampered with doubts concerning the nature of the limitation placed upon his actions by an intangible thing called a budget. The significance of this is incalculable. With the responsibility for budget administration you have in your hands the make-or-break of departmental management. I do not mean to imply that there are not other equally important factors—sound organization, for example—but it is quite clear that the art of getting the most inspired performance from men has, as one of its prime media of expression, the budget practice of the company.

BUDGETING IS THE EXPRESSION OF PLANNING

Thus far I have not done more than mention the controller and his place in this scheme of organized thinking. It is important that this be understood, but I should like to defer talking about it until we have considered the third law of budgeting which our company discovered in the search for knowledge in which it was perforce engaged. Stripped to its essentials, this canon says that budgeting is the expression of planning. Or, to put it another way, budgeting is the process of applying dollar requirements to an operating plan, piece by piece.

It goes back a long way, but I can remember when the word "planning" was never thought of in connection with the budget. The process we followed then consisted largely of estimating, for each expense account, how much more or less the forthcoming period would require than the figure for the immediate past period. Relatively little time was devoted to actually planning the operation, and, when subsequent comparisons were made of actual results with the budget, their value to management was proportionately diminished.

Just where in our history the planning idea was clothed with enough substance to make it effective in budgeting I do not know. Probably it was a gradual unfoldment. In any case, we ultimately evolved a new approach.

If the department to be budgeted was a production department, for example, we asked its foreman to think more deeply. First we gave him as clear an idea as possible of the job he was to do, including the probable range of volumes he must be prepared to handle. Then we asked him for a flexible plan. How much actual labor time per standard direct labor hour? How much setup and idle time? How much supervision? How much overtime and night shift time at various levels of operation? What percentage of material waste? What standards of maintenance? In other words, in terms of the operation itself, what is the plan for meeting the demands on the department?

The examples could be multiplied, of course, and the story is a familiar one to most of us. Yet it is surprising in how many places budgeting is thought of as a technique superimposed, rather than as the statement in dollars of a plan of operation.

There is also a deeper phase of this line of reasoning that ultimately makes itself known to the budgeting pioneer. Not only must the individual departmental budget be well grounded in planning; to attain maximum fruition the budget structure should rest on a foundation of planning which embraces every activity in the company.

PROFIT AND LOSS FORECAST

We have hammered at this fourth principle until we now feel that it is accepted by our management at all levels. The methods of applying it will differ in individual situations, of course. In our company we plan, budget and control by means of what is known as a profit and loss forecast for a period of twelve months ahead, and a financial program for a three year period. The former is revised quarterly, the latter annually.

The profit and loss forecast is simply the ultimate statement, in figures, of coordinated planning carried out in great detail by all units of the business. It starts with a forecast of orders received for each product and for each major market. When this part of the plan is approved—and this is sometimes a major hurdle in itself—we move to the Manufacturing organizations, where its Production Planning Department determines production quantities for the forecast period, as well as inventory quantities, with specific attention to leveling production over the period to avoid fluctuations in employment.

Responsibility for the prices applied to the quantities to be shipped rests with the Sales Division, although the President is the ultimate judge with respect to price levels. The Controller's Division then assembles all of these data and we now have a forecast of sales in units and dollars.

The Manufacturing Division furnishes us with all of the elements of the cost of sales figure—with the coordinating help of the Cost Department. This forecast includes standard costs and manufacturing variances, the latter in effect becoming a part of the planned cost of manufacturing.

To complete the picture, the other operating divisions of the company—the Purchasing, Research, Sales and Controller's Divisions—submit their budgets for the period. The general administration budget is prepared by the President, and the Controller prepares, subject to the President's approval, the budget of financial and other nonoperating items. Federal taxes on income are computed and we then have a complete profit and loss budget for the twelve month period. The entire process is repeated four times each year, providing each time a revision of forecast for nine months and a new forecast reaching three months ahead into the future.

The steps that I have described sound simple, and they would be if we ignored the quality and characteristics of the estimates entering into this pro forma profit and loss statement. The fact is that each determination has its roots deep in the procedure which we call planning, and this fact transforms the simple into the complex.

PLANNING A YEAR AHEAD

To plan a year of operations is practically tantamount to going through the entire twelve months ahead of time. All decisions must be foreseen and made. People must be employed and their compensation determined—all on paper. Negotiations must be concluded and contracts executed. New facilities must be provided if they are needed. It is no mean gymnastic to perform this array of tasks mentally in advance.

Furthermore, all decisions by an administrative personnel organized in the manner of these times into divisional, departmental or sectional units must be coordinated. Manufacturing must provide the quantities of product for which Sales takes orders, and Purchasing must procure the materials required by Manufacturing. Even Research is reduced to some scheduling, despite the well known maxim that you cannot timetable invention. It has been done, within limits.

Out of this welter of soul-searching, in which each man's plan is tested a dozen times and ways, and its rough edges worn off through multiple collision with the plans of others, comes that which guides the business. The master plan has emerged. Each part of it, a controllable segment, fits into place. The translation of this creature into dollars and labor hours and units of product is known as the budget or forecast. When the outcome has at last earned the blessing of top management and the Board of Directors, it becomes the guiding instrument for action.

I have tried in this brief description of our planning to illustrate a truth which, as soon as we discovered it, changed forever our attitude toward budgeting. It is so simple that, like any natural law, it hardly seems worth repeating once it has been mastered—yet it is fundamental. It is that the plan comes first, and the budget is no more nor less than the statement of the plan in all its facets in the common language of dollars.

THE FINANCIAL PROGRAM

This leads to a fifth point, although, chronologically, I am now less clear as to the exact sequence in which these were discovered, I suspect they were unfolding simultaneously. In any event, this one stands out sharply defined from the others.

We found that we must broaden the base of our planning to include a financial program as well as an operating budget. This conclusion could hardly be said to have come out of the budgeting project itself. It stemmed more from the absolute necessity of knowing what our cash balance would be three years hence if we committed ourselves to a large building program. It stemmed also from the need to know how much long-term money to borrow.

In retrospect, however, the entire conception of financial programming in our company bore a very close affinity to operating planning. Every accountant is sensitive to the interplay between operating and capital items. For instance, added to the legitimate reasons for replacing old equipment is the temptation to reduce by such a course the charges for maintenance and repair which seem to crawl upward with each year of a machine's life. To carry the matter a step further, it is probable that an organization with the best kind of budget control for operating costs but lacking control of capital expenditures will spend capital money unwisely. Feeling the healthy downward pressure on costs that such a budget system generates, it may find itself unconsciously saying yes to questionable capital expenditures, simply because new equipment of modern design usually cuts current charges to operations.

Our first step to extricate us from this trap was a procedure for appropriation, review and approval of capital expenditures. The Board approved individually all items in excess of $20,000, the President items from $2,000 to $20,000, and division heads items under $2,000. Many companies seem to have experimented with this type of scheme. Most of them I dare say have duplicated our frustrations with it. You are never quite sure you are doing just the right thing, even with a running total of approved projects to guide you.

Furthermore, and what was doubtless worse, there was never any reasonably reliable way of knowing how much we could afford to spend in total on the multitude of feasible sounding proposals which were always crowding in on us.

As I have said, the financial program, inspired by other needs, was taking shape meanwhile, and finally plugged the gap in our capital expenditure planning. It seems simple enough now, but it took quite a while for us to see that failure to plan completely will hinder the full expression of the planning idea in any segment of the company's affairs. To put it another way, the lack of a financial program, embracing capital expenditure planning, undermines the program of operating budgeting.

APPROACH TO FINANCIAL PROGRAMMING

I do not mean to imply that we are a model of perfection in this field, but to round out this picture, I should like to describe briefly our approach to financial programming. The complete program is constructed each year and presented to our Board of Directors at its December meeting. It covers a period of three years. Interim revisions may be made, of course, if needed.

Each division of the company is asked to submit for this purpose its capital expenditure requirements for the period, although obviously the Manufacturing Division gets the lion's share. Requirements must be detailed, by individual machines and pieces of equipment, and must be accompanied by information as to the probable date on which the cash disbursement will be made, allowing for procurement time. This latter fact calls for careful discussion between the Manufacturing and Purchasing Divisions.

The Sales Division is asked to produce a long range forecast, which sets the course to be followed with respect to products and volume. The Research Division is intimately connected with equipment needs for products to come. Nearly all of the operating departments of the company are involved in the process of thinking out the coming three years. Advance decisions are forced into being. The future of the company becomes a subject of searching thought. The eyes of the executive group and of many of their subordinates are turned to the horizon.

On this foundation, the Controller continues to build. Estimates of inventories during the planning period are elicited from Manufacturing. Accounts receivable are estimated on the basis of the sales forecast. Earnings levels are provided by the President. Depreciation reserves are computed, current liabilities approximated, and we now have the skeleton of a *pro forma* balance sheet for a period of three future years.

Only the cash balances and borrowings remain to be determined, and the decisions in this area are given top level consideration by those responsible. The three year financial program then takes final shape and, after approval by President and Board, becomes a fundamental guidepost. It controls the balance sheet in much the same manner as that in which operating budget controls the profit and loss statement.

Notice that we now have a control on capital expenditures at two levels. First, there is the list of individual items and projects which has been woven integrally into the overall financial program. Second, and particularly applying to changes in planning occurring as the year progresses, there is the ceiling on total capital expenditures in the financial program itself. The modern planning and control principle is given full expression through all the diverse channels of corporate activity.

RESULTS V.S. ESTIMATES

Out of all of this potpourri of thoughts emerges a sixth point to make note of in establishing the budget atmosphere. The success of a budget cannot be measured by how close the actual result approximates it. How many times have we heard sales executives chortling over hitting a forecast almost "on the nose"? Off-setting variations in individual products, markets, and prices may have been numerous and wide, but if the total sales figure for the month was close to forecast, the bright light of success is shining.

I should like to advance the thought that to exceed the sales forecast may indicate either good performance or bad forecasting; that to fail to sell the forecast level may indicate either bad performance or bad forecasting; and that to be under, equal to or over forecast may indicate nothing significant whatever with respect to the quality of performance or of forecasting. The last statement, of course, implies the appearance of developments which the sales executive could not have been expected to anticipate at the time the forecast was made.

Let us suppose, for example, that a new item is to be introduced to the line on a specified date. Let us further assume that we have a seasoned Market Research Department, which has studied the market potential by means of field survey and other techniques, and that the outcome of this study is a forecast sale of 5,000 units in the forthcoming year.

During the first three months, however, competition unexpectedly hits the market with a brand new feature, which temporarily paralyzes our sales effort. After 1,000 of the units have been sold, the item is remanded to Research for intensive study directed toward overcoming competition's advantage.

Now here is an unforeseen and probably unforeseeable development, which turns the forecast topsy-turvy. How much weight should we give this happening in appraising the quality of our forecasting? I should say none at all. Let us turn our eyes to the future, change our plan and move ahead.

REVISIONS—OR THE "NEW LOOK"

In fact this little example points up the need for a systematic method of revision for the entire plan—budgets and forecasts included. For the past seven years we have insisted on this "new look" four times annually. During the early part of this period we were more or less constantly working under the illusion that as soon as things returned to normal once more, we could reduce these revisions at least to twice each year. Now we know better. "Normal" is never coming back. In fact, we are a little doubtful if it ever was here at all. In any case, the pace keeps accelerating, new developments impinge on us with the speed of lightning, and we are more and more conscious of the need to be alert to shift our planning with equivalent facility.

It is this very flexibility in our planning techniques which holds our sights on the future. Comparisons of past performance with forecast are useful only as they guide us in our planning for the future. To put it simply, they retell us wherein we have departed from our plan, thereby affording us experience in the planning art.

If the planning was ably done and the control machinery well designed, these deviations were known before they occurred, and were based on appraisals and decisions made in the light of ample information, and in an unhurried atmosphere.

The crux of this entire argument must be apparent by now. The importance of having a plan is to provide some forward thinking to guide our decisions and to tell us how we are coming out if we follow it. If the pre-decisions are sound and the planning is based on all the available facts and on careful reasoning, it is a good plan. Whether we follow it or decide to change it is a secondary consideration, providing the change is made in an orderly manner. The one sin that we cannot afford to commit is to operate without coordinated planning. We may as well drive a car on a dark road at night without headlights.

THE CONTROL

My seventh and final point concerns controllership. I have reserved it until now because it is the catalyst. It activates all of the other organization factors insofar as planning and control is concerned. As a matter of fact, it is difficult to speak of budgeting without also talking about controllership because in a broad but what is to me a proper sense of the word, budgeting is synonymous with controllership. This is certainly true if we think of budgeting as the planning and control of an entire operation from stem to stern, including sales forecasting, cost and expense budgeting, profit planning, capital expenditure control, financial programming and so on. It is the controller, or someone with the controllership functions, who brings this thought-structure into being.

The first function of controllership, as stated in the Controllers Institute's definition, has received much attention in recent years. It might not be amiss to reexamine it in the light of our discussion of budgeting. It specifies that the controller is "to establish, coordinate and maintain, through authorized management, an integrated plan for the control of operations." It further says that "such a plan would provide, to the extent required in the business, cost standards, expense budgets, sales forecasts, profit planning, and programs for capital investment and financing, together with the necessary procedures to effectuate the plan." [*Editors' Note: see Exhibit 1 on page 18.*]

The particular point that I want to make tonight has to do with the controller's approach to carrying out this assignment. He must be endowed with a certain attitude which is not always easy to attain. We have heard much about his need to be placed at a high level in the organization, as a member of top management, and I think we have made substantial progress in achieving general management recognition of that fact. I am interested in equipping him with principles and an attitude with which he will be enabled to motivate his fellow executives toward a soundly planned, well controlled operation.

Properly speaking, a controller neither plans nor exercises control authority, except, of course, in the confines of his own department, where he is functioning as an administrator rather than as a controller. He does not plan for the company nor for any of its operating parts; his job is to see that the responsible executives do their own planning, and that they do it properly. He does not exercise control authority; he leaves this prerogative with those upon whom it has been conferred; his job is to see that they control their own operations.

Yet, in a very special sense, we may say that the controller controls. By that expression we mean that he provides the planning and control machinery and coordinates the efforts of the organization in using it. His work is a pure example of staff type activity. It is for others to do the planning, make the decisions, determine policy, issue and execute operating instructions and, in the long run, exercise control. But if any of these essentials is omitted or badly handled, the omnipresent controller is obligated to report the facts—diligently, decisively, diplomatically—to all levels of management concerned.

So let us consider this as our final gem of budget science for this evening—that the controller and his budget staff must control by indirection; they cannot issue orders nor make operating decision. By an inexorable law, each time they transgress this precept they pay corresponding penalty in loss of effectiveness. We cannot be all things to all men. If we are to cultivate a smooth planning and control mechanism, we must teach others to operate it while we carry out the selfless, service-motivated role usually referred to as coordinating.

The same advice may be given, of course, to cost accountants and other members of the controller's staff. Their task is never to censure, always to inform—never to veto, always to appraise—never to limit, always to support. Naturally, this group of men is looked to for a contribution to cost control, and the work they do in that direction is indispensable; but their entire effort should be directed toward providing the guideposts by which the responsible operating supervision may be assisted to perform creditably.

We might sum up the matter by saying that your budgets work best when the controller or budget man heeds the commandments we have been discussing. Budgets work best when he has enlisted the complete understanding and participation of top management in a planning and control effort which touches every phase of the operation. Budgets work best when the controller and his staff provide the inspiration, the machinery and the teaching for this process, but refrain from usurping the slightest decision-making privilege conferred upon their associates.

It seems a little ethereal to say that budgeting is a state of mind, but this is a conclusion which we are all forced eventually to acknowledge. It is an atmosphere and an attitude. It begins in the president's office (though the controller may have planted it there) and it trickles down through all the layers of the organization, until its laws are understood by the front-line supervisor, and even, to some extent, by the men and women we so easily refer to as "the workers."

Make no mistake—this state of mind is not one of niggardliness. It is not negative nor detrimental to progress. It is not one of pressure and friction, in which all are oppressed by a cruel philosophy of criticism in the effort to cut costs. All of these mistakes have been committed over and over in the development of this science.

Instead, the budget idea should invoke the voluntary self-discipline so necessary for accomplishment. It should promote the orderly consideration of problems when decisions can still be made ahead of time rather than in an atmosphere of crisis. It should help to fashion a structure of sound organization relationships, in which each manager or supervisor knows his duties, to whom he is responsible for their performance, and the importance of planning and control in carrying them out.

Based on the understanding and practice of good budget principle, there is no excuse for a budget system not making a surpassing contribution to the progress of any company. But we must keep always before us the fundamental that it is the human factor, properly evaluated and utilized, that makes a budget work.

CONTROL BY BUDGET [†]

by

James L. Peirce

BUDGETARY control has a thousand connotations, depending on the company in which it is practiced. The word "budget" alone has many meanings. Even the emotional responses it arouses differ quite radically. To some people it is synonymous with orderly management; to others it means restriction and frustration.

Many companies profess to have no budgetary control—yet upon questioning, their finance officers admit to multifarious versions of planning, estimating, forecasting and appropriating. These have a decided flavor of the budget despite all denials. It is a question, in fact, whether there is such a creature as a business without some form of budgetary control, or whether such an enterprise would not actually be out of control altogether.

This suggests the opportunity for some organized thinking in this fine field. It is my hope to survey with you a few of the difficult problems in which clear thinking is needed. Budgeting is a mature subject, and there is little really new to say about it. Yet its practice, on the whole, is not mature, and we all must face up to our failure to realize its full possibilities.

WHAT IS BUDGETING?

Is budgeting a mere technique or can we classify it as a science? Dictionary definitions seem to afford quite a lot of support for calling it a science. The presence of verifiable general laws and the systematizing of knowledge with reference to these laws is reason enough. I feel this to be important as a starting point. When fixed rules and laws can be discovered for the practice of any technique, it takes on aspects which portend great development. Budgeting fits this specification.

We find as we explore this subject that the rules which govern the science of budgeting are not accounting rules. Neither are they rules of organization, although both of these fields of knowledge are indispensable to

[†]Presented before the National Society for Business Budgeting. Reprinted from *The Controller*, July 1957, pp. 327-330, 352, 354, 356, copyright 1957, with permission of the Financial Executive Institute, 10 Madison Avenue, P.O. Box 1938, Morristown, NJ 07962-1938. (201) 898-4600. This article was also published in *Business Budgeting*, September 1957, pp. 5-12.

its practice. The rules with which we are concerned are those which establish working understandings between individuals.

It is only because business is a complex organization of many individuals that budgeting is needed. It makes possible the cultivation of the relationship of these individuals to each other along a constructive course. Budgeting is the most fundamental expression of the relationship of the man who hires to the man hired. It is a philosophy of communication.

To make this fact clear, examine for a moment, if you will, the ascending scale of man-to-man work relationships through the ages. The earliest (if we except involuntary servitude) was the simple agreement by the worker to do what he was told in return for a fixed wage. Later, a new incentive in the form of piecework found its way into the bargain. Then, as business advanced, came other incentives. In return for a man's best effort he was offered wage raises and promotions.

His performance under this arrangement was appraised largely on how well he used his employer's time. As his work began to include the supervision of others, it became important to consider his use of his employer's money also. It was here that the budget entered the scene. In one form or another his expenditures were planned and limited, and his success depended to a marked degree upon how well he handled the money allotted to him.

From this relatively modern plane it is only a step, although it may be a steep one, to the relationship which we are justified in considering the most enlightened yet discovered. Here management says to its subordinates: "First I will explain the job to be done. You plan it, with my guidance, and when I have approved your plan, we will agree on a budget to guide you."

Now we have the foundation of a sound business relationship between two individuals. The man responsible knows what is expected of him and how much he can spend. If circumstances change, a new budget may be built on the same foundation of understanding. But unless this occurs, the original budget is a commitment not to be exceeded without specific authorization.

Budgeting has become a management attitude. When line and staff understand it properly, the company benefits from constant attention to planning operations and controlling to the plan. A correct budget philosophy encourages independent thought and generates ideas. It furnishes the impulse to effective action and facilitates direction of executive effort. This spark of inspiration, however, comes not from the techniques of quantitative measurement but rather from the cultivation of a specific understanding between the man responsible for spending and the one to whom he reports.

WHAT IS A BUDGET?

The budget itself—the primary tool of this promising philosophy—may be defined as a plan of operation stated in the language of figures. It is also a constant look at the future—the beam of the headlight on your car. It is the indispensable preliminary to control. And it is the first essential of the incessant cost-reduction effort without which competitive industry could not survive.

In pursuing the definition of the budget, it may be useful to see what it properly includes. The first step is to recognize that it covers income as well as outgo. It is of little use to budget expenses without also budgeting sales, because the two are inseparably related, and must be controlled together. We will subsequently explore the close relationship of expenses and capital expenditures, and I hope to make it clear that the latter must be governed by a budget in order to make the operating budget work. It is only a short step to the planning of working capital needs and of financing, and when these have been translated into future dollar values, we may look at our planning and budget structure with a sense of completeness. We have an adequate tool for purposes of control.

Before entering into the details of the argument in favor of these conclusions, I should like to pose the classic issue that faces all who work with budgets—the question of what we might call its tightness.

How tight or how loose should a budget be?
Is the budget a standard?
A goal?
An estimate?
A maximum?
Is it normally attainable?
How does it relate to sales quota?
Or to forecast?

We have to deal here with semantics as well as concepts, but the distinctions suggested by these various terms seem fundamental to me. Some promising installations have degenerated until the budget has lost all meaning, solely from failure to maintain an understanding of what the budget level implies. Therefore our first need is to establish this definition.

THE BUDGET LEVEL

The budget level, as I see it, should always represent the actual plan of operations. The sales budget should express a planned level of volume. Cost and expense budgets should reflect amounts required to carry out a carefully constructed plan of production, selling, administration and so-on. The correlation is always to planning.

Yet we cannot stop here because planning itself requires defining. The planned level of sales, for example, is one that the company's best efforts may be expected to produce. It does not represent an easily attained minimum standard, nor is it an ephemeral goal, held always temptingly beyond reach. The plan is an objective that all who accept it can conscientiously commit themselves to meet by the full use of their energies. It is difficult enough to challenge but not difficult enough to discourage. It is rooted in prethinking so detailed and thorough that the organization knows, department by department, the steps it must take and the quality of performance it must display in order to fulfill it.

Now what about the related terms?

The word "standard" fails to convey the breadth of meaning that enters into a plan or budget. In currently accepted usage, the standard manufacturing cost of a product, for instance, may be a cost attainable under ideal, or even average operating conditions. It may be necessary, owing to unusual circumstances, to budget at a higher level than standard.

"Forecast" carries the implication of an appraisal of a future beyond our control—as we generally think of the weather. It loses the fine significance of specific planning and the clear mandate to provide the control feature. Looking ahead longer than, say, 12 months we might properly descend from budgeting to merely forecasting operations.

"Estimate" is subject to similar objections. It omits any sense of planning and control and leaves the flavor of guesswork. An estimate lacks conviction and character as compared with a budget if the latter is composed properly. It even suffers in comparison with a thoughtful forecast.

"Objective" is a word closely related to the budget, but its connotation is indefinite. We may have attainable objectives or deferred objectives, but the word has diverse meanings and is difficult to correlate directly with planning. The definition of our objectives is desirable, but we must then face the more difficult task of planning and budgeting to attain them.

"Goal" and "target" are useful words in the management process of building an organization's resolve for maximum performance. They lack the sense of obligation that accompanies a budget, however, and leave the implication of a desirable level, with some room for falling short of its achievement. Goals and targets have their place in budget practice. Particularly in long-range projection, they are valuable guides to progress, but the planning process transforms them into the solid reality of budgets.

"Quota," as usually applied to sales, is a selling tool. Frequently broken down into sales territories, it normally indicates an objective attainable with effort and experience. Quota levels vary widely, and are frequently the basis for payment of incentives. Quotas are commonly higher than budget levels, for a realistic sales budget necessarily takes into account any expected failure to reach quota in some territories. Furthermore the budget of sales volume must always be set at a realistic point in order that the budget of production may be established in conformity with it.

I am well aware that this vocabulary is not used uniformly in industry, and that shadings of meaning differ from company to company. Perhaps, however, this analysis will point up the absolute need for a concept of the meaning of the budget level in order for the budget idea to prosper in any organization.

THE VALUES OF BUDGETING

The heart of any consideration of the budgeting idea is contained in the values we expect to derive from it. We should therefore be devoting serious thought to what these values are and whether or not we are actually realizing them.

There are innumerable ways to describe the virtues of a budgeting program. Most of these advantages apply equally to a system of planning and control, for the two are really synonymous.

First in the list I should put the assurance that, if the budgeting is properly done and the control exercised intelligently, we have something approaching assurance of realizing a satisfactory profit. We need not labor the essentiality of a profit. Industry would soon crumble without growth and this growth is dependent upon a stream of new capital equipment, and this capital must, in the long run, be provided by profits. No business can successfully follow an unplanned, uncharted course. The present is one of the particular periods in our history when a profit cannot be realized without planning for it and exercising the controls that produce it.

Second, intelligent budgeting provides a basis for making proper management decisions. When a company's operations are geared to a preconstructed plan, decisions are not reached in an atmosphere of haste. Major decisions have been anticipated in the planning and it is possible at any time to appraise the effect of deviating from the plan. Such deviation may take the form of increases in wage rates, reductions in prices or failure to reach budgeted volume. Each of these occurrences, whether or not completely within the control of management, is made in relation to the planning, as evidenced by the budget, and its effect is reflected at once in revised planning.

The third specific value of budgeting derives from its use as a mechanism for controlling and reducing costs. The leverage of a planned profit operates to point up this necessity and emphasizes the rule of today's business that no continuing profit can be had without cost reduction. The budget should in itself call for a reasonable amount of cost reduction in each budget period. In fact it is almost certain that adherence to budgeted gross margin will dictate scrutiny of such cost-reduction avenues as improvement in manufacturing methods, reconsideration of make-or-buy decisions, reorganization of staff functions and so on.

The fourth value is a corollary of the one just mentioned. Budgeting provides a strong approach to controlling and increasing income. Proper sales volume planning calls for a well-designed campaign in each of the company's product lines and markets. Efficacious control would demand explanation and remedy for each deviation from planned volume as it developed. On signal, it would direct needed power to the vital income-producing phases of the business. At the gross margin level the budget program should point toward emphasis on relatively profitable items, simplification of product lines and design improvement to effect cost reductions.

THE DANGERS OF BUDGETING

Along with these values go some subtle dangers which deserve mention in order that we may be on guard against them. One of the most common of these is the failure to accept genuine opportunities because the costs which they entail are not provided for in the budget.

It is a reasonable guess that some companies will defer too long the installation of electronic data processing simply because its costs are not included in budgets. Product research is full of such pitfalls. The remedy is in a flexible attitude toward budgeting on the part of top management. A too rigid adherence to the budget may be shortsighted, when, with approval, it may profitably be exceeded or revised.

A corollary danger is the failure to reduce costs because expenditures are running within budget limits. It is very easy, for example, to fall into this trap: A budget of expense for the promotion of a given line of products is presented and its approval gained based on a well-argued case. Subsequent developments (such as delay of new product introduction) cause deferment of certain advertising expenditures. As a result, actual expenses for the department are below budget in total, and no effort is made to control or reduce the costs of the other items. The remedy for this and dozens of comparable situations is found in a management-promoted cost consciousness, applied unremittingly throughout the organization.

Perhaps even more costly than either of the errors just described is the possible damage to morale if budget administration is mishandled. When any manager fails to keep faith with a subordinate he is guilty of jeopardizing morale. An example of this is the tendency to ask for an all-out expense-reduction effort, to agree to the reduced budget so achieved, and then to insist forthwith on further reductions. Another sure way of creating trouble is to refuse an earned salary increase on the ground that it is not provided in the budget.

Only slightly less destructive is the across-the-board budget cut. When management decrees a reduction of, say, 10% in all budgets it confesses its inability to attack costs intelligently and to merit the cooperation of all department managers. The injustice and havoc brought about by the uniform-percentage cut is evident when we consider the differing characteristics of a company's departments. It may be feasible to reduce some by 15% and shortsighted to trim others by even 5%.

Another serious danger in budget activity is the introduction of wrong incentive. All budgetary control, measurement and standard-setting creates an incentive of some kind and the emphasis of that incentive must be studied with particular care. If a budget system reduces costs but fails to improve profit, we may have an example of improper incentive. A sales department devoted to low-cost selling but ignoring the potential volume in the quantity-buyer market which requires higher caliber salesmen is misplacing its emphasis. A management dominated by the index of return on investment may be blinded to opportunities offering only moderate profits but with important future possibilities.

Examples could be multiplied, but these mistakes will suffice to point out the element of danger in the budgeting process. This is a powerful tool and it must not be misused.

WHO MAKES THE BUDGET?

The starting point for sound budget practice is the placing of responsibility for making the budget. We have long since discarded the crude beginnings of budgeting in which a foreman was handed a complete budget to govern his operation, put together by a staff department or by his boss, without his participation. We have, in fact, almost accepted the broad principle that he ought to prepare his own budget. This advanced stage of delegation, however, can only be reached when he has a thorough knowledge of the job to be done, some expert guidance from his superior in the performance standards he should be expected to achieve, and help from a skilled budget staff.

Given these conditions, the foreman should be in a position to do his own planning, and hence to prepare his own budget. Collaborating with the factory superintendent, he produces a budget satisfactory to both. From this point, combined with the approved plans of other foremen, it enters into the total budget for the manufacturing operation.

Assuming approval at the level of management responsible for profits, the budget then becomes in effect an authorization to proceed in accordance with the plan. The budget is in fact nothing more than the orderly statement of the plan—in dollars, machine-hours, units of production, manpower and so on—arranged in such a manner that it may be compared with actual results in convenient time spans.

Although this planning initiates with the foreman or department manager, it should be emphasized that the budget cannot be prepared successfully without strong initial leadership from management in setting operating objectives. This factor should be introduced at an early stage in the process of budget making. It also demands a background of education in company policies under a continuing program. The exercise of management guidance is not inconsistent with the principle of requiring a foreman to make his own budget, but rather should insure a result more in harmony with the profit objectives of the company.

In making effective the principles we have been discussing, a few simple rules of procedure must be observed. The first of these is: Only charge to a man's budget that which he can control. There are of course varying degrees of control, and a charge for floor space, for example, is a legitimate cost of the operation of a department manager, even though he may not be in a position to control the elements which comprise it. But meaningless lumps of uncontrollable apportioned overhead serve no good purpose and tend to mystify and discourage the manager.

Particular care must be used in charging for services performed by other departments. There must be available to the manager so charged an explanation of the services he receives in sufficient detail that he can exert his effort to keep them at a minimum.

Finally the accounting used for budget purposes must be clear. The accounts must be well defined as to content, and adequate explanations of amounts over or under budget must be supplied promptly. These are self-evident rules, but they are too often disregarded. The resulting confusion will nullify the value of the budget system.

BUDGET CONTROL POINTS

In the timing of budget administration there occur a number of specific points of contact and decision involving a manager of a budgeted unit and the man to whom he is responsible. It is extremely useful to identify these key occurrences, which may well be referred to as "control points." They are the specific times when, under the design of the plan, management effort is exerted in the planning and control process.

We have already discussed the first control point—the original construction, review and approval of the budget. The second is deviation from the budget, a control point which comes into focus in one of two ways. The preferable way is through seeking approval in advance for the deviation. The other is through the post-period comparison of actual results with budget.

The challenge to strong budget management is to equip the manager with sharp enough tools and to train him sufficiently in their use, so that he can recognize imminent changes in cost levels in time to report them in advance of their occurrence. If, for example, an increase in production load will obviously cause the department to incur some overtime premium cost, it should be possible to recognize this in advance. Coming changes in personnel, in products or in machines used are frequently known. Weekly production and efficiency reports provide knowledge of deviations from budgeted levels without awaiting the monthly budget comparison. A manager attuned closely to his operation and familiar with the make-up of his budget is currently aware of his budget status.

The significance of this technique as a budget control point lies in the use to which it is put. It is here that control is exercised. Budget is not exceeded except by approval, even if the excess cost is unavoidable. By organization steps the deviation travels up the line until it reaches the lowest level at which the decision can properly be made. In cases of substantial variations or sizeable accumulations of small variations, this point may be the president's office. The magnitude of the effect on profits is the determinant.

The understanding governing the company's budget program should provide for full discussion of instances where exceeding expense budgets would seem to be to the benefit of the company. Permission to do so should be forthcoming if it can be demonstrated that such action will be profitable.

The third control point is revision of the budget. This is a topic in itself. Before considering it, we might well examine the timing of budget operation, since the cycle adopted materially affects the revision control point.

Allowing for differences in various types of business, it is probably reasonable to apply the term "budget" to a plan which extends for a period of no longer than one year. For such a period the budget may normally be prepared in as much detail as required for control purposes, although the latter portions of the year need not be supported immediately with complete detail.

For the following two years, generally the planning is more of the quality of an "estimate" or "forecast" than a budget, and one of these terms would be preferable. This period should normally call for a sales forecast, an estimate of profits, and a financial program which includes planned capital expenditures.

Beyond three years, the quality of the planning is such that it might be termed a "projection." Long-range forecasts of sales volume and of capital requirements are of value in picturing the future growth and other characteristics of the company and in visualizing capital needs.

BUDGET REVISION

The basic fact to deal with in considering budget revision is that conditions change. Sometimes the change in outlook is radical and rapid; at other times it is gradual. Both adjustment to external changes and internal improvement require shifts in planning, however, and the budget must be as flexible as the plan. We must have an orderly process for its revision.

How flexible can a budget be?

At one extreme we might subject it to continual revision, perhaps even monthly, reflecting each failure to sell or to contain costs. This is a weak approach and does not emphasize adequately the necessity for living up to commitments. At the other extreme we might conceive of operating for an entire year with no revisions. Experience with this method shows that as the months go on changes in conditions and related changes in planning render the budget unrealistic. Both extremes destroy the effectiveness of any budget.

The occasion for revision is more a matter of management judgment than of formula. I think we must start with the premise that no revision should be made in volume or expense levels unless our considered judgment tells us we must abandon the original plan. In such an event we ought to have positive reasons for making the change, or else prove to our satisfaction that the original plan itself was wrong. Major changes in markets, products, prices or wage levels would naturally call for revision of budgets. If the budget is to be maintained as an active, live instrument of control, it must be kept current.

Since top management is responsible for the net profit of the company, it must be aware of changes in planning at any level of organization which affect that result. It follows that any occurrence bringing about the need for budget revision is a concern of top management and should be given consideration at that level. Budget revision therefore finds its ultimate in the budget profit-and-loss statement, comparing new with superseded planning, and providing management with the means for placing divisional and departmental responsibility for the changes.

Countless techniques are practiced for revising budgets. The most common timing appears to be a quarterly revision. Some companies revise for the remainder of the calendar or fiscal year—others for a new period of 12 months reaching into the following year. Still others leave the original budget unchanged and carry a parallel running estimate, revised frequently, in order to appraise and control deviations from budget. The particular method adopted does not appear to be as important as it is to exercise correct budget principles to effect control.

BUDGETING REQUIRES FINANCIAL PROGRAMMING

One of the really significant advances in recent years in this science is the developing recognition that planning and control, and hence budgeting, cannot be restricted to operations but should embrace capital items as well. Not only capital expenditures are included in the coverage of a sound budget program, but every item in the balance sheet. This conclusion at first seems radical if you have not followed through the chain of reasoning which supports it, but is readily demonstrable and has been proven sound in practice.

All financial management will concede the necessity of planning ahead for capital requirements. Forthcoming needs for plant expansion and increases in working capital items accompanying growth in sales volume furnish reasons aplenty for careful scrutiny of future needs. Since the period of planning for this purpose is normally longer than one year, let us refer to the plan and its statement in dollars as a "financial program" rather than a budget.

Strangely enough, such programs, in various forms, have been employed for many years by the financial officers of many corporations, while at the same time an operating budget was used by a controller or chief accounting officer for the current control of expenses and profits, without any conscious coordination between them. Modern planning and control demand that they be coordinated.

It is interesting to note how well the budget principles already discussed fit this pattern. Assume, for example, that we are constructing a financial program for a manufacturing company for a period of three years. The first step is the preparation of a detailed budget of capital expenditures for the first year, together with estimates of requirements based on production planning for the two following years.

The first year's budget should include a listing of individual machine tools, equipment and capitalizable improvements. It should be prepared by manufacturing management, placing ultimate responsibility at the lowest practical level. Coordination by staff engineering departments should not be permitted to obscure the basic responsibility of line management for this budget, since the latter's use of the new equipment will have a direct bearing on its operating budgets.

The second and third years' needs may be estimated by manufacturing management, with participation by plant superintendents, central manufacturing executives and staff engineering groups. Approval is ultimately required, as for the operating budget, at the top-management level.

The procedures for approval of capital expenditure budgets, reporting of expenditures against budget and revision of budgets differ in form but not in principle from the manner of handling operating budgets. The control points are the same. So is the basic organization relationship that gives life to the budget idea.

The incentive for control is somewhat different, however. Whereas the need for adequate profit impels the control of operating costs, another motive appears (aside from the relatively minor depreciation charge increase) for avoiding wasteful capital expenditures. Lack of control will create excessive capital investment on which an earning is required. Although each capital expenditure proposal may meet the formula test of prospective net return, experience proves that advance planning, budgeting and control is also needed as a brake on a mounting capital investment.

Furthermore, close budgetary control of factory operating costs will create pressure for capital items. Most new machinery purchases are justified in part on the basis of improved speed, capacity or accuracy, all of which are usually translated into reduced costs. It is obvious that in a factory where heavy pressure is exerted on costs without comparable control of equipment purchases, capital investment will tend to increase excessively.

CASH CONTROL

The capital expenditure budget and forecast having been established, we can complete the financial program for the three-year period. Broadly speaking, this falls into two parts: requirements for capital, and sources of capital. These, of course, correspond with the assets and liabilities sides respectively of the balance sheet. For this reason it is sometimes simplest to approach the financial program from this standpoint, although various kinds of cash flow budgets are in use.

Visualize, if you will, pro forma balance sheets at the close of each of the forthcoming three years and at interim dates during the first year. First a cash balance should be provided which will serve the company's normal operating needs. Receivables and inventories may be estimated based on anticipated turnovers related to forecasts of sales volume. Fixed assets are determinable from the capital expenditure budget and estimates just described, and depreciation reserves may be fitted in [calculated] based on current rates. Any other assets which are a part of the company's operating picture are added, and the total of requirements for capital at the close of each year of the program has been projected.

On the liability side, accounts payable, accruals and tax reserves may be estimated, leaving only the sources and amounts of capital to be supplied. The earned surplus account will be a composite of the current balance and future estimated earnings, deducting anticipated dividend declarations. The balancing figure is the amount of capital required to be furnished by equity investment and by borrowings, both long- and short-term.

We can now bring into focus two very important objectives of this extensive planning, and perhaps from the point of view of financial management, these are the epitome of the entire process. One is the capital structure to be employed and the other is the control of the flow of cash. The two are closely interrelated.

The space at our disposal does not permit a survey of the factors which govern the choice of sources of capital. It is elementary that the rate of earnings on equity capital is normally improved by the use of the company's credit in arranging long-term borrowings. Short-term loans may then be fitted into the picture to provide cash for temporary peak requirements.

In considering any channel for securing money, profits are of primary importance, for it is this yield which services the debt—both income and principal. In planned profits are found interest and dividends as well as repayment of loans.

I hope this chain of thinking has spread before you the panorama of budgeting in its larger significance. Budgeting was once a term which referred only to a technique for the control of costs and expenses. Today its meaning has broadened until it has merged with the idea of planning and control, embracing income as well as outgo; the longer foreseeable future as well as the period just ahead; the financial program as well as the operating plan. I have tried to make plain the close interrelationship of these areas of thought and to show that eventually, in order to do the right kind of budgeting job, we must include them all. No part of the program may be omitted without jeopardizing the whole.

COST REDUCTION AND THE BUDGET

I have referred to the fact that continuous cost reduction is indispensable to industry. This point seems worthy of special emphasis. Cost-reduction programs, in various forms, have become a significant factor in the ability of many companies to stay in business and make a profit.

Now the budget has been a primary tool of cost reduction. It has furnished a guidepost from which to seek and measure cost savings. Some companies have successfully employed a cost-reduction budget, by which is meant a goal of specific savings accumulated through the organized efforts of line and staff groups. The savings are costed and accumulated statistically without regard for the offsetting effect of any cost increases occurring at the same time.

Regardless of the cost-reduction technique employed, regardless of whether the factory or the office is the target of cost-reduction effort, the budget is the starting point. This purpose, however, sometimes causes conflict with the concept of the budget as a planning instrument. To treat the departmental expense budget, for example, as an approved plan, does not encourage further cost-reduction effort.

The challenge is to use the budget intelligently for both purposes—or, perhaps better stated, to identify the two purposes with each other so that they become one.

Ideally, in the process of setting budgets, we should give full scope to all the techniques of measurement. The budget should reflect a plan free from excess costs, trimmed to the point where to abide by it and turn out the work requires all concerned to be performing at a creditable standard. Thereafter the effort should be to control by variance from budget, under the well-known principle of management by exception.

If a standard-cost system is used, it will frequently be necessary to budget variances from standard. An example is the excessive material cost anticipated during early periods of production of a new item. There are many other instances where we must expect and therefore plan for excessive costs, perhaps of a temporary nature, which should not be incorporated into the standard cost of product. Here the management-by-exception spotlight would fall on the excesses over budgeted variances.

As a practical matter it is difficult to rely wholly on the management-by-exception theory because we are never completely confident in the budget itself. Therefore in searching for the maximum yield of which the organization is capable we apply our measurements to actual results. This is almost the sole reason, for example, for comparing this year's sales with the same period of last year. If we were fully confident in our budgets such comparison would be of little value; previous experience would have entered into the budget of sales so that we would only be interested in comparing actual results with budget.

I think it is evident that we will never lose interest in the year-to-year comparison. By the same token, regardless of the care with which the budget has been constructed, we must take advantage of the additional dimension provided by measurement of actual against actual—for examples, the useful ratios of sales expense or of research costs to sales volume.

The cost reduction effort then must be pursued comparing today's costs against previous performance and against such goals and standards as we can develop to measure operating efficiency, as well as against budget.

It should be self-evident that the presence of a plan ought not to be allowed to vitiate the force which might exceed it. It is one of the particular responsibilities of management to be alert to avoid complacency in those areas where the budget is being met, when additional effort might produce an even better job.

THE CONTROLLER AND THE BUDGET STAFF

We have discussed at some length the particular line relationship that gives the budget its vitality. I should like to refer now to another working understanding, equally important—that of the budget staff to the line. This contact point may well determine the degree of success achieved by the budget program.

No written job description can do justice to the qualities a staff budget man must have, nor to the attitude he must display toward those responsible for spending. He can neither censure nor praise, being obliged to leave these offices to line management. But through his skill in measurement he may help them to a self-appraisal. He may not dictate budget levels, but the force of his staff assignment will contribute generously toward establishing them. He may not interpose himself between the line manager and his boss, but he must be aware of all that transpires in the operation of which they are a part and be alert to the opportunity to motivate them constructively toward a well-planned and firmly controlled operation. He is in short an expert in minding his own business while at the same time making everyone's business his own.

In this sense, the controller himself should be the chief budget officer. He not only defines the required attitude for the entire accounting and budget staff, but he exemplifies it in his work at the top-organization level. The management function exercised in the president's office should be augmented by the budget practice known as controllership.

The first function of controllership, as given in Controllers Institute's definition [*Editors' Note: see Exhibit 1 on page 18*] is worth re-examining in this connection. It states that the controller is "to establish, coordinate and maintain, through authorized management, an integrated plan for the control of operations." It further says that "such a plan would provide, to the extent required in the business, cost standards, expense budgets, sales forecasts, profit planning, and programs for capital investment and financing, together with the necessary procedures to effectuate the plan."

This statement epitomizes the planning and control idea. It expresses the delicate distinctions which the controller must recognize in all his work. Coordination must be effected not through any authority of his own to issue orders, for he has none, but rather through the line management so authorized. Note, too, that the controller does not maintain the control of operations, but only a plan for such control, thereby leaving the control itself in the hands of those same authorized individuals. Finally, the techniques of control, such as standards, budgets and forecasts, are properly made the means for control rather than ends in themselves.

The second of the controller's stated functions is "to measure performance against approved operating plans and standards, and to report and interpret the results of operations to all levels of management." The statement, again subordinating means to objective, goes on to specify the techniques included in this assignment—namely "the design, installation and maintenance of accounting and cost systems and records, the determination of accounting policy and the compilation of statistical records as required."

The reporting and interpretation called for in this function are an important part of the budget program. They should be observed at all levels of budget practice, the controller's office being the source from which the philosophy emanates.

By the terms of this definition we have now established the place of the administration of planning and control in the organization. It is laid at the controller's doorstep. His is the task of disseminating this idea, with its unlimited possibilities. With only staff authority to represent top management in the planning and control area, he finds his most effective weapon to be the power of the idea alone. If he learns to use it well, his business will realize a sense of direction that can only result from adequate planning, accompanied by control to the plan.

The controller then truly controls, in the very special sense of the word that budgetary control implies. He provides the planning and control machinery and coordinates the efforts of the organization in using it. It is this sense of control that gives life and meaning to our budgets, and elevates them to recognition as a powerful force for industrial progress.

EMERGENCE OF THE FINANCIAL EXECUTIVE

THE NEW IMAGE OF CONTROLLERSHIP †

by

James L. Peirce

THOSE who have followed the development of the controllership image during the past three decades have been deeply impressed with its vigor and breadth, as well as the rapidity of its acceptance. They have witnessed the coincidence of management's hunger for controls and the upsurge of an eager and articulate group interested in designing and furnishing them. The practitioners of this new art have experienced the consummate satisfaction of making a heavy contribution to the greatest industrial growth in history.

For 31 years this movement in management has been fostered and led by Controllers Institute of America. At the members' meeting on April 30, 1962, this organization, at a high point of prosperity and reputation, adopted a new name: Financial Executives Institute. This change is significant to business in the United States and Canada. It is doubtless of ultimate importance to business in other countries as well. It is symbolic of a metamorphosis in corporate organization. It signalizes the triumphant conclusion of the development phase of controllership and the initiation of a period of greater maturity, power and recognition.

The action referred to reflects in part a tendency for industry to integrate its financial functions in a single top level executive. It would be a serious mistake, however, to conclude that the image of controllership is to be subordinated or diminished. Controllership is the practice of the established science of control. Its definition will grow sharper and it will be better understood by all financial executives. It will be specifically applied by a controller, or in some cases by a staff officer of some other title, but it will henceforth be a primary concern of every leader of a business organization.

MP&C THE EPITOME OF CONTROLLERSHIP

The allied area of planning is also the concern of controllers, but in a less direct way. The absolute indispensability of planning to the control process involves the controller in every aspect of planning. It is axiomatic, and now generally accepted, that the planning function and the control

---

†Reprinted from *Financial Executive*, January 1963, pp. 13-15, 19, 36, 38-39, copyright 1963, with permission of the Financial Executives Institute, 10 Madison Avenue, P.O. Box 1938, Morristown, NJ 07962-1938. (201) 898-4600.

function are forever wedded. This truth has given rise to the commonly used phrase "Management Planning and Control."

It now remains to be made equally clear that management planning and control is the epitome of controllership and that the abbreviation MP&C is the symbol of the principles under which controllers operate. We are seeing a new image of controllership and can well devote some time to thoughtful analysis of the words "management planning and control." As financial executives and practitioners we must understand them clearly. Moreover we must prevent their being misused by our associates in management.

"Management planning" comes first. This is a widely respected term and one that is subject to many interpretations. Nearly everyone in management acknowledges the value of planning but there is a diversity of opinions as to what it means. Let us draw at least the broad lines of definition.

Management planning begins with objectives and purposes. This is always true, even though they may never have been reduced to writing. It is far better, of course, that they be recorded. This is the orderly way to initiate planning, but most of the time we find management's objectives hidden in the minds of management. Then too there is sometimes quite a disparity between the various objectives cherished by individual members of the management team.

Before we go much farther we must clarify the meaning of "objectives." Objectives are not the same as plans. We determine objectives first—then devise plans to meet the objectives, or sometimes to go only part way in meeting them. Then we translate the current portion of these plans into budgets. A budget is the organized expression of planning. Budgets and plans are closely allied. They are on the same level. Objectives, on the other hand, may be far beyond planning and budgeting. The same is true of quotas, targets and goals. These all represent that which we are aiming to reach. Planning and budgeting, however, must be governed by realism.

LONG AND SHORT RANGE PLANNING

These terms are so often confused that an example may be useful. A company's long range objectives may include: achieving a position of leadership in a given field; gaining a foothold on foreign shores; diversifying product lines; decentralizing operations; or doubling in size. Its shorter range objectives might include: improving gross margins; eliminating unprofitable product items; increasing sales volume by a given percentage; reducing operating expenses to a given figure; or achieving a specific net profit return.

Long range objectives require long range planning. Take, for example, the first mentioned objective: achieving a position of leadership in a given field. Planning to meet this objective might involve: specific provision for engineering of improvements into product; new approaches to attaining customer acceptance through advertising; reorganization of the marketing structure; or acquisition of patents or manufacturing facilities. Also, during this process we become more specific in quantitating our planning. Planned unit and dollar sales volume for a five year period, for example; projected additions to the sales force; footage of needed new plant area; timing of product introductions—all may be part of the long range planning process designed to meet the adopted objectives.

Short range planning is more detailed. Let us look at one of the examples of short range objectives given above: improving gross margins. Planning for this objective might well include: a specific program of cost reduction; planned selective price increases; or development of new sources of supply for purchased products. At every step the construction of this planning will demand to know how much, when, where and who.

Moreover, it must be well thought out. It must be documented in detail and supported with plenty of figures. It requires the participation of every responsible operating and staff manager. It cannot be left to chance or based only on hopes.

Too often management has hopefully permitted an estimated percentage reduction in costs to creep into planning without doing the necessary hard thinking on the steps to be taken to realize it. This overoptimism then moves from plan to budget, and the cost of the error is sacrifice of confidence in the budget itself. Lacking respect, the budget, like a dull cutting tool, is worse than none at all because it results in spoiled work.

This is a good place to integrate capital planning into our structure. It is self-evident that planning—even for the shortest period—could not be complete without specific provision for capital expenditures. There is a saying that when you push down on costs, up pops a capital expenditure and vice versa. This is reason enough for controlling both at once, but there are other reasons. Investment demands a profit return—whether it be in equipment or working capital. Even the coveted sales increase will generate more receivables—hence more capital on which a yield must be earned. Projections of capital needs must be built with the same care, under the same principles, and usually at the same time, as operating plans.

MODUS OPERANDI OF CONTROL

We now come to the subject of "control." There are a great many kinds of budgets in use today in industry. They vary in quality from the refined and sharp instrument, skillfully used to channel the organization's energies into profit-making, all the way down to the sledgehammer pounding at operating expenses.

An operating budget is the short range profit plan of the company, stated in money and other units. It should rest on well constructed current planning covering every organization unit in the business. And the planning should rest on stated short term objectives, which in turn are a segment of long term objectives and related long term planning. Once you have embraced the management planning idea, there is no stopping point short of applying it to every action, decision and policy of the business.

Control is the twin brother of planning. The two are interdependent and neither can function without the other. Control is the tool of presidents—not only of controllers. It is the philosophy and action which keeps operations in line with planning; or explains, preferably in advance, why operations must deviate from planning; or enables management decision to deviate intelligently from planning.

The budgetary science is grounded in principles that are so well known that they hardly need restating. They were formed during the forties; hardened and polished during the fifties. In the sixties they will be employed with more skill.

For instance, we are learning that control to a plan is not enough. It must be supplemented by the periodic revision of the plan itself. When any aspect of the plan becomes obsolete, it is to that extent no longer valid for control purposes. For example, when a product is discontinued, the resulting reductions in promotion costs cannot be labeled as savings against budget. This fact, so simple as to be hardly worth mentioning, is often ignored by controllers, forgotten by presidents, avoided by sales executives.

Again, control mechanisms cannot be limited to comparisons of results with budgets, and current decisions with plans. Other devices of control must be in the tool kit. Measurements in terms of operating relationships must be kept sharp and in use. These, familiar to all, include: percentages of categories of expense to correlated sales volume; ratio of indirect to direct labor; return on capital invested; and many others. The mature executive—line or staff—will keep unremitting vigil on the trend of these indexes, and will give constant thought to the perennial question: What should this standard be? He will constantly probe the thinking of all subordinates for soft spots which reveal potential improvement—entirely apart from the guidelines of plan and budget. This too is control.

All of this shapes up into a sophisticated organization concept, typified by the question: Who exercises control? Who impels and applies this power? The answer has become clearer in theory with the passage of time, and, in some cases, very definitive in practice; in many others the practice is cloudy indeed.

We have obviously been describing a top level function. Further, this is basically a line function, vesting in the executive head of the business. It is then delegated to the line executives and, functionally, to the control staff. The extent to which control coordination can be delegated by the top executive is the form and outline of a creature referred to as a controller.

Let us recognize here that there are many true controllers and many financial executives who perform all or a part of the controllership duties under various other titles. Therefore we shall be referring, when we use the term, to a man who has these responsibilities, regardless of his title. In like context, when we refer to the president we mean also, when the occasion demands, an executive vice president or even a general manager of an integrated operating division.

Since the controller is a staff executive and cannot issue orders to the vice presidents in charge of sales, manufacturing, research, he operates his domain with a mixture of salesmanship, service motivation and vested functional authority. Skillfully employed, this formula is highly effective, particularly when supported by an enthusiastic president.

Specifically, the controller designs and installs the control system (including the use of budgets, measurements, standards, accounting, reporting and related techniques) and then proceeds to coordinate its application. His sphere of activity is well established; has been published for many years; and has, on the whole, been accorded acceptance by industry, writers on management, the schools and management engineers. It reaches a peak in charging the controller with the duty of consulting with all segments of management responsible for policy or action concerning any phase of the operation of the business as it relates to the attainment of objectives and the effectiveness of policies, organization structures and procedures. This is broad scope for one man.

RESPONSIBILITY FOR PLANNING

But if we have opened wide the controller's doors to the upper realms of management thought, we have withheld one critical duty from him. He is not responsible for planning. He is not, strictly speaking, even eligible to coordinate planning, though the wording of the statement brings him within a hair's breadth of this duty. It asks him to coordinate a plan for the control of operations—not a plan for operating the business. The distinction is fine but important. Obviously there is no control without planning, but the planning itself is to be done by others.

If then, control is to be provided by the controller, who is to provide planning? A planner perhaps? I am not proposing the introduction of such a title, but industry has begun to exhibit here and there a new executive sometimes referred to as Planning Manager or Vice President-Planning.

Here we are faced with a familiar problem. To what extent can the president delegate the planning function? Perhaps we have a logical parallel with control. We have already noted that control itself, in the line management sense, cannot be delegated to staff but that the coordination of control can be effectively conferred on a controller. Let us examine the possibility that, similarly, planning itself cannot be passed on to staff, but that the coordination of planning may be susceptible to delegation.

The organization of the planning function in industry is certainly in its infant stages when compared with the present development of the control function. At the current pace, however, another decade will witness its maturity. Controllers will have a finger in determining the direction it will take.

This leads to another interesting field of thought—the affinity between control and capital management, and the marked tendency of late to merge the two under a top financial executive. Sometimes this executive has the earmarks of a controller, as we visualize the prototype, but he has some such title as Vice President-Finance. In the larger companies he may have both a controller and a treasurer reporting to him.

The history of corporate officialdom sheds some light on this trend. Anyone who can look back over fifty years of business can recall the day when it was customary to provide a president, a vice president, a secretary and a treasurer in each corporation, although this arrangement varied somewhat with local laws. In due time a second vice president (or even more) began to appear but the treasurer was always the officer responsible for finance, including raising and collecting money and, as a kind of sideline, keeping the books as well. In the United States, the event that signalled the beginning of a new era in accounting took place on March 1, 1913, when the first corporate income tax law became effective.

Gradually, as tax rates increased and everyone became aware of the need for more exact determination of net income, accounting began to take on the characteristics of a science in its own right. The treasurer found himself with a trained chief accountant on his staff and forthwith relied on him more heavily for facts about the business.

The president and vice presidents began to rely on him too, and to go to him directly for information—partly because he had it and the treasurer did not, and partly because there were a great many treasurers in business who held that title as watchdog of large shareholders or lenders, and were not familiar with the minutia of the business.

METAMORPHOSIS OF THE CONTROLLER

It is probably not possible to pinpoint the first appearance of the controller. The name, previously comptroller, is an old one, derived from the French. Its root form is the equivalent of counter-roller, or one who kept the count in the roll form of antiquity. Suddenly, in the twentieth century, in the mysterious manner of word-fashion, the title leap-frogged over accountant and achieved executive status. The vogue developed during the twenties and by 1931 there were enough controllers to form an Institute in New York.

The new organization spread and grew. It satisfied the needs of myriads of men, young in spirit, ambitious, accounting-trained, tasting the first fruits of recognition in a new management function. And management needed controllership. The complexities of New Deal social legislation, the mounting burden of taxation, and the sharpening of competition all contributed to the need. Not only were the controller's cost systems and figures in demand, but his judgment also, and in the top councils of the business. Treasurers either learned the new function themselves or, more often, moved over to make room for the newcomer.

Controllers Institute of America in 1961 celebrated its 30th birthday, with 5,000 active members, all of executive status, 54 local units, a headquarters office and staff, a separate research foundation and a monthly magazine. During this 30-year period the Institute became the headstone of industry's house so far as the planning and control idea is concerned. It developed and disseminated a careful statement of controllership functions; and through its conferences, its magazine and innumerable talks given by members and others, it advanced the new MP&C techniques to a point of widespread acceptance. The Institute does not claim to be the only source of original thinking and educational effort on this subject; but it lays well-founded claim to being the leader in the field.

A principal contributing reason for the Institute's phenomenal success has been its persistence in researching and explaining the MP&C philosophy. The literature it has poured out on this subject is voluminous, and the round table and conference discussions, were they to be recorded, would be even more so. Looking backward, it seems clear that the central characteristic of this group for many years was that it simply would not let this subject alone until it began to emit the light of wisdom. Even today, the research foundation is embarking on a momentous project, the purpose being to construct an authoritative statement of MP&C principles.

The steps of development we have been describing are interwoven with manifold changes in concepts of organization. In many companies controllership duties have been integrated with those of treasurership. Defining the latter is not difficult owing to the weight of supporting tradition. Their core is the procurement of capital, but the treasurer also determines capital requirements, collects accounts, invests funds and supervises the effective use of capital generally. Unlike controllership, this sphere of operation has always been recognized as the concern of top managements and Boards of Directors.

A few years ago the prophecy was widely entertained that controllers (as distinguished from controllership) were destined universally for top level organization status. The events of the past decade have altered this course. Many treasurers are responsible for the controllership duties, either personally or through a subordinate controller. In some cases also we find treasurers reporting to controllers and, in fact, an infinite number of variations of these arrangements.

There is today a strong current running toward a single top finance function, embracing both the controllership and the treasurership duties. We now have the reincarnation of the treasurer of a generation ago, but clothed also with the newer responsibilities of control. He is usually a vice president and in the larger companies may be found supported by both a treasurer and a controller.

It is precisely for this reason that the Institute has graduated to a new name and scope. Membership is now attainable under either of dual sets of specified duties—one defining controllership as in the past, and the other specifying what constitutes treasurership. Thus the long period of integration which has been taking place in industrial organization thought has been formally recognized.

Nevertheless the two functions are quite distinct. This fact deserves all the emphasis we can give it. Regardless of the organization design under which controllership and treasurership are assigned, each contains elements peculiar to itself and not held in common with the other. Controllership must be viewed as grounded in management planning and control; treasurership in the function of providing and managing capital. Each gives rise to its individual philosophy and practice. Both reach independently to the realm of concern of the president and board of directors. Each maintains its own distinct image. The current trend toward combination of the two under the organization classification of finance must not be permitted to obscure this salient point.

THE CONTROLLER IDENTIFIED WITH PROFITS

Having identified controllership with the MP&C idea, we may now probe deeper into the motivation behind the idea itself. This leads directly to profits. All planning, all control, all techniques of measurement and budgeting are shaped to this end. Hence the controller's image in the minds of business management and public is that which most vividly represents profit realization. In terms of the annual report to shareholders he is Mr. Net Income. No one competes with him for this title—not the treasurer, nor the sales or engineering executives, nor, for that matter, the president himself, who perforce embodies the personality of the company as a whole.

Because controllership is thus identified, it becomes the obligation of controllers to be protagonists for profits. They may find it necessary to clarify the matter of why adequate profits are so desirable. There is ample evidence of misunderstanding on this point. How can we hope to set a profit goal and then gear the organization through MP&C to proceed down this road unless all concerned have a clear idea why profits are needed?

All of us are familiar with the studies of public reaction which show that the average person has an exaggerated notion of the profits earned by large companies. This illusion may not be swallowed by so-called "middle management," but another one, equally vicious, is frequently entertained even by this group. I am referring to the common misconception that the main purpose of improvement in earnings is to increase dividends. The fact is that profits serve two purposes: growth and return on capital.

126

A little reflection will show that these purposes are more closely intertwined than is at first apparent. The demands of growth raise the louder voice. Earnings retained in the business are the foundation for growth. They permit expansion of sales volume, acquisition of new products and facilities, modernization of plant and all the other steps that forward movement requires. Even more important, this capacity for taking advantage of such opportunities, of itself, removes the shackles from the responsible executive group. It extends horizons and encourages the initiative that is so essential for progress. By the same token, the company's growth becomes the growth of the individual.

The element of return on capital is also important. Dividends exert a strong effect on the attitudes of stockholders, and a pattern of dividend stability and increase has a bearing in the financial market place on the company's leverage in raising new capital. This is in face of the fact that undistributed earnings increase equities and offer a limited class of shareholder the attractions of capital gains. We must conclude that even income influences growth, since the maintenance of securities markets, buttressed by solid financial public relations, keeps the door open to new capital when it is needed.

The line of reasoning we have just outlined should be the controller's key to establishing firmly in the minds of management at any level the need for an adequate profit. Profits mean growth. Growth cannot be had without profits. Individual growth cannot be had without corporate growth. And we can neither attract nor retain competent management without individual growth. Net conclusion: without profits the business ultimately loses its identity. In today's atmosphere, unlike that of the thirties, the process of attrition is not permitted to run its course to receivership; it stops when the business is sold to another company which recognizes the importance of profits and is willing to do what is necessary to produce them.

It is surprising how often these basic facts of corporate existence are either unknown or ignored. They should provide controllers with a strong foundation for the case they must make for MP&C.

Having recognized the supreme need for profits, what is the most productive way to achieve a profitable operation? What is the road to profits? Would it sound too obvious to say that we must plan for profits and then control our operations for fulfillment of our plans?

CREATION OF THE PLAN

Many thinkers arrive at this point. Few carry the idea to the action stage. The task of creating a planning structure where practically none exists seems staggering at first. The very process of reaching agreement within management, at points where agreement is absolutely indispensable, is a formidable one. Sometimes it is difficult even to harmonize views on stating the questions to be answered.

Now contemplate an operating plan for a period of three to five years ahead; varying appropriately in the degree of detail included for the years covered; filled in with sufficient policy and operating decisions to make it a practical guide; and capable of revision as dictated by current developments. Visualize a statement of broad company objectives with respect to products and markets, with supporting summaries of the actions required to attain these aims. Include in your mind's eye a tabulation of dollar sales volumes by major product lines for the next five years; projections of plant and equipment investments and plant loads; estimates of working capital needs; and estimates of amounts and sources of capital. Add too a statement of marketing objectives; a list of sales outlets in all parts of the world in which the company expects to do business; a tabulation of numbers and types of required marketing personnel. Then flying in the face of all that appears to be impossible, develop a picture—rough though it must be—of the categories of new product and improvements in product which research may be expected to offer.

The foregoing can only be suggestive of course. The form that planning will take must vary with the individualities of companies. It must be created by staff personnel close to the president, under his devoted direction. It must be hammered out of the dissensions and diverse experiences of the executives responsible for sales, manufacturing, research, personnel and finance. Only in this way can a document be assembled which is the embodiment of realistic planning.

Further, it must, when faced with defeat on the field of specifics, retreat to the realm of broader policy. This phase of plan architecture demands skill, tenacity and diplomacy. Degree of detail and sharpness of focus must be carefully graded downward as the period of projection lengthens.

So far as the advantages of planning are concerned, it is hardly necessary to recount them. Everyone has his own way of stating the virtues of planning. One manner of summation of advantages might be as follows: (1) planning forces thoughtful consideration of objectives, both long and short range, and therefore brings a sense of purpose into management thinking; (2) planning harmonizes the actions of the various elements of the business and therefore brings a sense of unity into management thinking; (3) planning provides a structure of predecision which guides management toward its goals and therefore brings a sense of direction into management thinking; (4) planning underlies control, which in turn brings a sense of disciplined action into management thinking; and (5) planning produces profits and therefore brings health and growth to the company.

Beyond all of this, management planning, time-consuming though it may be, results in a net saving of time in the long run. One company's management recently devoted the best part of many weeks studying the possibilities of acquisition of another company, only finally to reject the proposal for reasons which should have been understood at the outset. The merger would have brought together operating units and product lines too diverse to manage effectively together.

The penalty could have been even worse, of course. Some managements have found it costly and painful to untie a knot which was tied without enough preliminary thought. They have been the victims of the merger and diversification fever of the past few years. Clear statement of objectives and sound long range planning would have protected them from such experiences.

THE CHALLENGE TO CONTROLLERSHIP

The road to profits is strewn with the wreckage of vehicles which were too weak to endure its hardships. We seldom hear of the ventures that have failed. We seldom take note of those which, though still in existence, move along at a crawling pace, yielding no satisfying result. The diagnoses of the ills that have caused the demise of business enterprises seem simple in retrospect and their transgressions sound avoidable with common sense. Yet many of those same patently wrong decisions were carefully made in the light of the factors then apparent.

How many of them could have been avoided in the presence of genuine planning? How much loss could have been prevented with proper control? These questions cannot be answered with precision. But experience points the finger at haphazard operating and decision-making, and the handwriting is already on the wall. Wages increase and prices hold firm—and many a management, faced with the inexorable demand for profits generated by a growing business, squirms as the pressure mounts.

The planning habit, like the control habit, is difficult to inculcate. It is difficult beyond the conception of most of us. Sometimes it demands a cataclysmic change in lifetime habits of thought. It involves the daily relationships of people in all levels of supervision. It must combat the competitive pressure of massive demands on everyone's time for the solution of today's problems. Even with the most sincere intentions (which are not always present) and the most profound devotion to the idea on the part of top management (which also is not always present) the task is still a staggering one.

Yet a look about him will reveal much upon which the controller may build. He will find, if he looks for them, evidences of planning in the recesses of his associates' thinking. He will sometimes discover a refreshing eagerness to be directed into the intelligent use of MP&C. He will see in use various techniques which harmonize with the theory of planning and which are only awaiting an architect to fit them into the whole structure.

The new image of controllership is seen squarely in the framework of management planning and control and of profit realization. These constitute his mission, his guiding motivation. He is the stimulus of planning and the fountainhead of control, and if he allows them to fall into disuse, he has ceased to have a reason for being so far as his company is concerned. Accounting, important as it is, must be considered an auxiliary technique, as are taxes, integrated data processing and all of the other time-demanding activities that flood his office.

Controllers have before them a work of transcendent importance in the practice of their trade. This work requires vision and singleness of purpose. It is no mean career to live up to the promising image which they themselves have created.

BUDGETARY ACCOUNTING AND ITS PROSPECTS †

by

James L. Peirce

AT the turn of the century, accounting was primarily a record-keeping function. Fifty years later it had become the primary tool for the control and direction of industrial enterprise. Budgets had come into maturity and were widely used in successful businesses. There was an extensive literature on the subject, the antipathy of managers to this form of control was diminishing, and the principles of planning were being widely studied and applied.

Now the winds of change are again sweeping through the twentieth century. A kind of revolution is taking place—or perhaps, better said, a series of revolutions—in automation of production processes, in acceleration of the pace of research, in the remodeling of marketing methods, in the shattering of old limitations in data processing. Moreover, industry worldwide is responding to a demand for higher standards of living than have ever been dreamed possible in all the history of mankind.

The consequences of this upheaval are vibrating through the accounting profession. The maintaining of records of operating results, and even the determination of net income, important as these duties are, have made way for a new assignment. Industrial accountants are being enveloped in scientific planning and control. Accountants today are more and more identified with management, furnishing and operating the machinery of control, penetrating into the secret recesses of the operating plan, and revealing the precious fact that lights the way to management decision.

The identifying characteristic of the new and exciting face of accounting is that it looks into the future more intently than into the past. It is this attitude which distinguishes budgetary accounting and justifies the subject of this article. It is my aim to point out how purposeful is the commitment in this direction on the part of industrial accountants who are in tune with the flow of modern management thought. By the same token, in discussing budgetary accounting, we are primarily concerned with the accountants of private industry (whether manufacturer, retailer, utility, or bank) rather than

†This article is based on an address at the Ninth International Congress of Accountants, Paris, 1967. Reprinted from the *Financial Executive*, February 1968, pp. 66-70, 72, 74, copyright 1968, with permission of the Financial Executives Institute, 10 Madison Avenue, P.O. Box 1938, Morristown, NJ 07962-1938. (201) 898-4600.

with public accountants or those in government. These men bear the responsibility for carrying the principles and techniques of planning and control to new heights, and with this development, for equipping industry with the sense of direction which it will need in the last and perhaps most agitated one-third of a turbulent century.

MANAGEMENT VIEWPOINT

The viewpoint required to assimilate and reflect the spirit of modern budgetary accounting is completely identified with management. What management must have in order to manage becomes the dominant objective. This fundamental rule cannot be overemphasized. For an accountant to emigrate, as many have, from the familiar surroundings of profit-recording to the pioneer land of profit-making requires courage and mental stamina. To serve management with the unique skill that marks the seasoned control staff, accountants must think as management thinks.

As a basis for considering the nature and *modus operandi* of budgetary accounting, let us further examine this matter of management viewpoint. At the very heart of management's commitment is the demand for growth in the business. Growth is profitable to the ownership, which is management's employer. Furthermore, growth is an instinctive urge in men of managerial calibre, and, therefore, the personal aims of the individual and those of his employer are wholly compatible. The natural form in which this motivation expresses itself is profit realization. Earnings retained in the business are the foundation of expansion of sales volume, acquisition of facilities and product lines, and of most of the other steps that comprise forward movement.

In the sharp emphasis on profit which this reasoning generates, we cannot ignore long-range corporate health. It may be shortsighted, for example, to defer research, institutional advertising, pension programs, and educational and scientific donations in the interest of current profits. These expenditures represent essential investments in the future. They express the view that long-range profitability can best be promoted by creating a profitable transaction for the customer, a profitable working climate for employees, and a profitable relationship with the surrounding community, whether this be provincial or worldwide.

In the framework of this discriminating profit emphasis, then, falls the proper operating attitude of management, which the accountant must adopt and absorb. Driven by the urge for profits, accountants have largely designed and promulgated the budget idea. Impelled by the management principle, they have carved out workable organization arrangements in which they act as staff to management, coordinating the budget system without direct line authority through the weight of the service they perform, the knowledge they possess, and the confidence they have earned from management at all levels.

PLANNING AND CONTROL

It is of the utmost importance that accountants assigned to staff budget activities understand clearly the principles and practice of what has come to be commonly known as "planning and control," whether applied under that name or some other, such as the "budget system," "budget control," or even simply "budgetary accounting." As in any discipline, the rules are simple of statement and easy to adapt to practice, but they have been widely misunderstood and hence misapplied.

Assume a factory department responsible for a certain type of machining. Its foreman is informed by responsible supervision (in this case, the factory superintendent) of the kinds and quantities of work that will be required of the department during the year. On this basis, working with the budget accountant, he prepares a plan of operation.

In theory this step precedes the preparation of the budget, even though in practice they may be done simultaneously. The foreman at this stage is encouraged to recognize that he is responsible for performance in accordance with plan. He should also realize that changes in the company's operating planning may alter his budget and that unforeseen circumstances may require him to seek approval to exceed it. The proper degree of and emphasis on budget responsibility is supremely important to the planning process.

The planning having been completed and the resulting budget approved, the control phase is begun. It is here that the exact relationship of plant superintendent, foreman, and budget accountant must be understood clearly. This triangle is characterized by freedom of communication in all directions and by fidelity to the functional parts to be played by the three individuals. It is this typical segment of organization structure that practices the principles of control and that determines the success or failure of the budget itself.

During the early years of development of this concept it was useful to dissect the control relationship and to identify such elements as reporting, decision, action, revision of plan, and so on. Advanced management has by now absorbed this analysis into its thinking and seems ready to turn to the more complex concept of the control process as a whole.

Reporting, for example, is seen as a continuous mental process, assigned in this case to the budget accountant, and carried out with the intensity of the beam of a searchlight. Reporting takes various forms. Periodic reports, containing both figures and comments, may be monthly, weekly, daily, hourly, or, more likely, a combination of these. Reporting is also oral and timed to the needs of the occasion. Its subject matter may be performance in total against a budget figure, a measurement against a standard, or a critical appraisal of the standard itself.

It is evident that a reporting assignment requires insight and tact. There is one cardinal rule, the breach of which may destroy the budget accountant's usefulness: all pertinent facts must be reported, even though in different form or detail, to both the foreman and the superintendent. The latter must not be equipped with operating information not available to his subordinate.

The foregoing triangular pattern is repeated as many times as there are units of responsible supervision in the company. The influences here described multiply into a control mechanism which covers the entire operation, and the identical principles apply at the highest level. The process is continuous and simultaneous, not spasmodic or sequential. A management in tune with the planning and control concept is constantly planning, the budget staff is exercising the control function without interruption, and the decision making, despite its inherently painful problems, moves forward in a clearer light than could ever be possible without the planning and control foundation.

From this background emerges the branch of accounting that we call budgetary accounting. It should now be evident that its rules are found more in the behavioral than in the quantitative techniques.

CONTROLLER AND HIS STAFF

It was inevitable that the planning and control idea, gradually growing into the acceptance and prominence that it now enjoys, should remake the structure of business organization. A staff executive was needed who would be responsible for coordinating control, but not for any operating duties except to maintain an accounting department. This man is called the "controller."

The use of this word as a corporate title has generated a great deal of controversy. The implication that a controller should, in fact, actually "control" has given rise to much misunderstanding. It has not been easy to bring about general recognition that the word "control" is here used in a special sense which has nothing to do with the direct authority associated with ownership or line management. The term here refers to the special assignment of providing authorized management with the planning system, the standards, the budgeting, and the interpretive reporting necessary to guide a business on a profitable course.

It has become customary for the controller to report either to the top executive officer of the company or to a top financial officer. There are many variations in practice, both in organization design and in duties. In particular, the duties of controllers and treasurers are frequently interwoven. It is clear, however, that the controller must have direct access to the chief executive officer of the business and must enjoy his complete confidence in order that the man responsible for the operation of the enterprise may have uninterrupted illumination of its affairs as well as the all-important levers of control. In a degree these specifications apply also to the members of the controller's staff in their conduct of the control apparatus in their respective spheres. The controller and his staff are a unified group, activated by identical principles.

It has been well established that to operate effectively a controller must at a minimum coordinate an integrated plan for the control of operations. This task must be performed through the individuals authorized to conduct operations. The line organization issues the necessary commands; the controller and his staff must conduct an educational campaign to explain and motivate the use of adequate planning. They must then exercise the vital control force in a completely indirect manner through the action of responsible line management.

The unique position of the controller in the organization affords a hint of the massive and unrecognized power that resides in this assignment. Its potential contribution to appraisal of the performance of all functions of the business and to a realization of profit opportunities is almost unlimited. As with all positions of great trust, it also contains within itself the possibility of abuse, and it must therefore be exercised with integrity and objectivity.

Budgetary accountants may well heed the complex nature of these relationships and the demands which must be satisfied by anyone who would aspire to the delicate task of applying "control" without direct authority. Controllership is the epitome of the budgetary science, and in some degree its principles are practiced by accountants at all levels in any company which relies on a budget system.

RESPONSIBILITY AND ACCOUNTABILITY

In order to construct an operating plan suitable for the purposes of budgetary control, the presence of certain attributes of sound management must be assumed. One of the most indispensable of these is a clear definition of responsibility and a correspondingly clear conception of accountability. The operating responsibility of any manager should be stated in writing in unequivocal terms, and the authority for action with which he is endowed must be as clearly delineated.

The first ingredient is the determination of the specific objective of the department under consideration. This, of course, can only be done within the framework of the broader objectives underlying company planning. The department manager should then take a major part in determining the amount of expenditure required for its accomplishment. This phase may involve the reconciliation of his views with those of the man to whom he is responsible. It gives rise to cost-saving opportunities of the utmost importance to the forward motion of any company. Such possibilities should be carefully appraised and incorporated realistically into the planning. When agreement has been reached, the budget is approved subject to final approval of the planned profit result by top management.

The degree of commitment to an approved budget then becomes an element in the organization structure exerting an important bearing on the success of the company. A manager's commitment should be either to accomplish the desired and approved objective, at the cost provided in the budget, or to explain satisfactorily why it will not be done.

The word "satisfactorily" in this context means much. The failure to realize budgeted sales volume would demand accountability as the circumstance developed rather than mere justification at a later date, and to exceed budgeted expenditures would require authorization in advance. Either of these happenings could be expected to initiate full executive review if profits were materially affected.

The concept of accountability of management has already exerted an important effect upon accounting classifications. A budget-controlled company cannot afford such a traditional catch-all as a large and elastic general administration expense. Depending upon the nature of organization responsibility, we are now likely to find this category divided into such groupings as treasurer's department, controller's department, industrial relations department, planning department, and so on. The expenses of each manager who is held responsible for performance must be recorded as a distinct budget unit, and all expense items must be assigned to the lowest echelon compatible with decision making.

By the same token, this concept leaves no room for large apportionments of various kinds of overhead expenses merely to impress the departments concerned with the magnitude of administrative costs. Only specific services rendered by other departments justify inter-departmental charges; in such instances they should adhere to organization lines.

PLANNING PROCESS

Since budgetary accounting is closely allied to planning and budgetary accountants are forever identified with the planning procedure, it may be useful to review briefly the steps in the planning process, with particular reference to their significance to the future development of the profession.

The first step is the establishing by executive management of a foundation for the planning phases to follow. This step is indispensable. It consists of the determination in advance, in consultation with the principal operating and staff executives, of the general objectives for the year or other period ahead and the means to be used to meet them.

The second step is the creation of a rough picture of a future result. Sometimes referred to as a "profit model," this states, in a minimum of words and figures, the most reasonable projection of sales volume, costs, expenses, and profit that can be constructed. Its purpose is the provision of early guidelines for all major segments of the company and to introduce prior to the detail-planning stage the self-examination and explanation that invariably accompanies the construction of new programs.

Third in logical order is a tentative agreement upon levels of income and expenditure between the top executive and his operating subordinates. At the conclusion of this step, the skeleton of the plan is outlined. With the coordinating skill of the controller, the profit plan is being hammered into finished form.

The fourth step is detailed planning. At this stage the control staff is introduced more completely into the project and each manager prepares his budget and discusses it with the man to whom he is responsible. The accountant assigned to carry out the staff control function specifies the form of accounts to be used as well as the supporting detail to be furnished. He points out the opportunity for cost saving but makes no decisions concerning either the plan or the budget.

The fifth step is assembly by the control or accounting staff of the composite operating budget. Every phase of accounting required in the recording of transactions and the determination of net profit is also required in the budgetary projection for the year. For example, rates of depreciation, provision of reserves, valuation of assets, and provision for contingencies must all be predetermined. Budgetary accounting, therefore, has become in this sense the image of actual accounting. In the design of the system of accounts, however, the reverse is true. Actual accounting must be the reflection of budgetary accounting.

The sixth and final step is executive review and approval of the budget by the top management of the company. This step requires discussion and frequently adjustment of plans and budgeted amounts before final approval is given. The *modus operandi* involves participation, individual creative planning, responsibility, and commitment. The process of budget-making within this framework establishes and reinforces the essential stature of a manager and provides him with a climate which encourages his growth. It releases the latent capacities of men to achieve the maximum result for the company.

FUTURE OF BUDGETARY ACCOUNTING

Strictly speaking, there is no such thing as budgetary accounting. The sciences of accounting and of budgets, much as they have in common, are distinct. Accounting must always be concerned basically with the statement of fact (the determination of net income, the valuation of assets, the specific cost of products, for example) whereas budgetary science is made up of the techniques of planning a business operation and of providing the controls which will make it possible for management to operate profitably in relation to its planning. The viewpoints of these techniques, their rationale, principles, and methods of application are essentially different.

This clearly defined separation does not apply, however, to the individual members of the accounting or budget staff of an industrial company. It is self-evident that budgetary practice demands accounting training, and it appears to follow from this that accountants are best qualified to become budget practitioners. This is further borne out by the widespread concentration of budget staff responsibilities in the departmental units responsible for accounting.

A budget accountant, however, must be far more than an accountant. A controller is far more than an administrative accountant. The budget and control attributes and responses are more related to the organizational and human relationships between people than to the figures themselves. The presentation of the budget idea to one's associates in a manner that enlists their cooperation, the cultivation of constructive attitudes toward the use of budgeting as a management and operational tool having real value, and the creation of a motivation for budgeting which is free from the abuses which abound in practice are needs indispensable to success.

This discipline suggests the outlines of tomorrow's development. Planning and control principles will be more widely applied as the pace of business continues to accelerate. The time has gone when a company's management was able to recognize a change in the business atmosphere by observing its effect on daily affairs. At today's speed of movement, the beam of the headlight must be projected farther on the road ahead. The race for markets will leave behind those who fail to plan intelligently and to practice control in the modern sense of that term.

It will be seen more clearly that business can and must provide budget staff service to design reporting which will point out and emphasize only that which is significant and omit the masses of irrelevant figures which can now be produced with such ease with data processing equipment. The budget staff must appraise the specific need of each operating manager and meet it with the custom-built product.

CONTROL OF CAPITAL

Another clearly predictable trend is the wider application of planning and control principles to the use of capital. It is being demonstrated more emphatically than ever before that the amount of capital employed in a business is a critical element in its success. Now as always, the demand for a reasonable return on capital and a satisfactory growth in the investment originates with those who supply it. This is the natural and eternal stimulus to effective use of capital. The only difference between today's conditions and those of past times lies in the intensified competition for available capital. Adding to this influence is the heightened alertness of professional investors in large mutual and pension funds.

With this new interest in capital demand, supply, and use has come a sharper focus on measurement of return on capital and a more critical appraisal of investment opportunities. Within companies having decentralized operations has appeared a new emphasis on return on investment as a measure of profitability and hence as an ultimate criterion of effective performance. The return index may be computed for each subdivision of the business sufficiently distinct to justify individual accountability for profit.

The ratio of return, usually computed as the net income, before taxes on income, divided by the average value of assets employed, after deducting valuation reserves, has to a great extent become the epitome of investment performance measurement. To a management with eyes on this index, all efforts to increase it work together in the direction of preserving, benefiting, and augmenting the business. We have already discussed the numerator of the fraction (net income) and its susceptibility to the relatively sophisticated planning and control science of today. The denominator, although equally important, has enjoyed less attention. The control of the amounts of capital employed offers a major opportunity, therefore, to improve the return on investment.

In creating the mechanism with which to accomplish this purpose, cash balances may be subjected to control standards by determining for each depository bank the amount of the minimum balance which will normally reimburse the bank for services rendered plus a reasonable profit. Accounts receivable may be broken into geographical and market categories, with indices of turnover and appropriate standards computed for each category. Inventories may be successfully budgeted for as long a period as is covered by current operating planning, with monthly budgeted amounts established for all major categories of inventory.

Capital expenditures should be budgeted to the divisions and departments of the business requiring them. This budget is determined in close correlation with operating plans and is approved and administered under the same principles. Individual projects and equipment items should be budgeted for a period of one year and the control effort exercised at the point at which the expenditure is authorized. At that time, all of the techniques of appraisal, including economic computation of savings, may be brought to bear on the decision.

Finally, the complete capital program, including both capital required and its sources, must be brought within the principles of planning and control in order to assure the company's management and directors of sound financial guidance. The various types of assets—cash, receivables, inventories, and so on—together with the current liabilities, debt, and capital accounts, may all be included in a composite plan, ultimately expressed as a projection of future balance sheets. It is normal to prepare such programs to cover a longer period ahead than is practical for operating budgets—for a period of three or five years, for example. It is the specific opportunity of accountants in industry, working hand in hand with responsible management, to carry the financial or capital planning to such a point of completeness that every element of capital, as well as the operating budget itself, fits consistently into the total picture. Only in this way can the power inherent in the planning and control idea be fully realized.

CONTROL OF RESEARCH AND DEVELOPMENT

The last area of business operation to come within the boundaries of control is always research and development. It is natural that this should be so. From our laboratories come the products that shape the future, and it has long been alleged and accepted that invention cannot be shackled with time schedules and price tags.

But the growth of dependence on research and the fast competitive pace of product change have elevated both the importance and the cost of the research effort. This new conspicuousness has generated a demand for closer correlation of research expenditures with the commercial objectives of the company. Closely following is the inevitable insistence on control. Here is an urge to improve, not just control of the expenditure of funds, but control of the direction of the work itself. Management needs to know that research projects are pointed toward profitable goals rather than goals considered interesting by the research staff.

It has long since been proven that the costs and expenses incurred in a research department can be collected for these projects, and that periodical reporting can be made accordingly. The real test of the budget accountant, however, lies not in these areas but in the effectiveness with which the budget is used.

It is a characteristic of the research activity that it normally operates at a relatively stable level of employment. New personnel is usually added only in response to rather specific needs, normally well planned in advance, and there is little current variation in the salary accounts in total. Staff time, however, may be distributed very differently between projects from period to period.

If the control of research through its budget is to be effective, the aim must always be control of research objectives and of progress in meeting them. Top management should first establish the direction of the research effort. This being done, it becomes possible to agree upon budgeted project costs. Reporting on achievement, however, must be qualitative as well as quantitative. It must indicate the current status of each project in relation to its objective. It is not enough to know the extent to which actual project expenditures have varied from those anticipated in the planning stage.

This realistic reporting suggests a relationship involving the research executive and the top operating executive of the company. At this point the technical appraisal and the financial appraisal come together. At this point also the flow of funds to research projects is controlled.

More and more, the larger companies are assigning to the research activity full-time budget accountants charged with the responsibility of understanding the activity as fully as possible, of assisting the research staff in the practice of budgetary control, and of coordinating actual reporting with progress reporting by research personnel in such a way as to make possible intelligent decisions respecting the flow of money to research projects.

DATA PROCESSING DEVELOPMENTS

There can be little doubt that the techniques of data handling are in the midst of the most significant revolution ever witnessed in this field and that this development will also have some impact on budgetary science. There is more room for doubt whether, as has frequently been held, it will produce changes in the principles of business management as distinguished from the practice. A serious temptation is evident in the literature of the times to assume that the radical changes in method now taking place signify fundamental changes in philosophy.

The opposite view, perhaps too conservative, is that the impact of electronic data processing on this decade is of no different magnitude than the impact of punched-card tabulating on the hand posting of accounts in the twenties. Punched-card tabulating refashioned the techniques of recording and reading out the statistics of business. It was accompanied by significant forward movement in management thought, such as that leading to the unfolding of the planning and control idea, but it is difficult to reason effectively that the two forms of progress were interdependent.

There is no doubt that today's almost unbelievable acceleration in the pace of data processing and the ability of current types of equipment to turn out details in forms and combinations hitherto impossible have sharpened the available accounting tools and contributed greater accessibility of facts to the planning process. These, however, are changes of form rather than of fundamentals.

One of the fields that appears at this time to hold promise of more basic forward strides is the use of computer equipment in the construction of projections of the future, sometimes referred to as models. Corporate planning inevitably takes the shape of product planning, since the introduction of new products and the modification of old lines is at the heart of industrial progress. The product model, projecting volumes, prices, costs, margins, and all other elements bearing on profit, has possibly opened the door to a new era in decision making.

The special aspect of this technique that justifies the effort and expense of computer application is the ease with which the model can be altered. Once the model is programmed, it is a relatively simple step to change it in manifold ways and provide a printout for purposes of management consideration. Various mixes of product, combinations of prices in different markets, varying cost assumptions, and so on may be applied to the model, and the profit result measured under any combination of assumptions desired.

The ability to manipulate a planning model with a computer opens the door to a new world of ready responses to what might be called "if ... then" questions. (If one variable in the projection be altered, then what is the effect of this change on the whole and on its parts?) Accountants accustomed to the flood of such questions often asked by operating or general management will welcome this development. It is within the capability of the computer to add a new dimension to the familiar product projection and thereby to exert a material effect on the planning decision.

SUMMARY OF OUTLOOK

The future of budgetary accounting is already determined by the shape and magnitude of the forces operating in the industrial and economic scene. To meet the demands on the free world in the surging evolution of this century, business will depend more than ever before on planning that is both creative and painstaking, and on control that is both firm and sensitive to change. The accountants of a few years ago who have had the insight to grasp the meaning of this development are today's controllers. The present practitioners of the budgetary art will one day be guiding management through clearer and more orderly processes of decision making. More specifically, the outlook for this disciplined state of mind and technique that we refer to as budgetary accounting may now be summed up as follows:

1. The budgetary accounting phase of the current revolution in management technique will accelerate. Eventually most businesses operating under a free-enterprise profit system, and many operating under other systems, will find the use of budgetary practices essential for survival. Control to pre-established, although flexible, planning will be nearly universal among successful industrial companies.

2. Budgetary accounting is likely to dominate all industrial accounting. It will no longer be merely a branch of accounting, since the techniques of net income determination will receive less management attention then the applied principles of planning and control. As a result, internal accountants will be more identified with the actual operation of the business—its products, its research, its marketing, and so on—and therefore even more welcome in the councils of management decision.

3. Accountants, particularly those directly concerned with the budgetary control process, will increasingly turn their eyes away from the past and toward the future. In a staff capacity, they will take part in the construction of the plan itself. There is no other equally qualified and objective group within an organization to whom management can turn for this kind of trained viewpoint. Since a budget is, simply stated, the quantitative expression of a plan, this opportunity will come to accountants quite naturally.

4. Accountants will enter more positively into the indispensable cost control and cost reduction effort. It is a basic responsibility of line management to apply cost reduction pressure relentlessly. The budget accounting staff can materially augment its contribution to the company by providing the motivation for this effort as well as the systems of reporting and recording cost reduction achievements. This arrangement need not

vitiate the authority of direct operating management, but, properly used, should provide it with valuable measurement tools.

5. Control of the use of capital will assume a place of importance equivalent to control of net income results. The growing relative scarcity of capital and the competition for return on its investment has already begun the destruction of complacency in this area. Every asset on the balance sheet will fall under increasing scrutiny as accountants turn to the serious application of budget principles to the allotment of capital. Planning, measurement, and control will be exercised here as vigorously as on costs of production.

6. Accountants skilled in budgetary science will devise means for controlling research and development expenditures more effectively. This will be impelled by the needs of industry, which is pouring massive and increasing amounts of money into research, much of it still inadequately planned and out of the effectual control of general management. The competitive demand for new products and product improvement will make it clear that top management must have its hand firmly on the direction of this activity, and this can only be accomplished through more scientific planning and budgetary control of research direction and projects.

7. The main impact on budget practice of the data processing revolution now taking place is likely to be in the construction of flexible models for the planning of operations. The use of complex net profit projections for individual product lines or for the business as a whole, with multiple adjustments of variables to reflect alternative volumes, prices, costs, marketing methods, and so on, give promise of sharpening the planning process. The much-quoted advantage of sheer speed in computing periodic results may be expected to accelerate the pace of business operation rather than to change it basically.

THE CHANGING FINANCIAL EXECUTIVE †

by
James L. Peirce

IN the tangle of conflicting ideas that seems to be gripping our best thinkers today—in industry, finance, government, religion, or whatever field you can name—there emerges one refreshing area of harmony. Everyone seems to be in complete agreement that we are in an era of rapid and radical change. If there is one word, in fact, that characterizes the entire scope of humanity's thinking today, "change" seems to be that word. We hear it constantly at professional conferences. We read it in business literature and in the annual reports of corporations. We hear it thundered down by congressmen and generals, glorified by management consultants, and repeated in swelling volume by business executives everywhere.

HOMAGE TO CHANGE

We are in fact not only in the midst of one of the most intensive periods of change in our history, but we have established a fad of change to which we pay fairly universal homage. Change for the sake of change has become for many a guiding star, and I have noticed that some of us have been all too happy with simply staying in motion, whether or not alteration of our course is really profitable. Furthermore, we have generated in some quarters such a fear of remaining static that we have sometimes discarded well-tested principles for inferior substitutes. It seems to be the mark of alertness and vision to be advocating dynamism and innovation with all of our force, and most of the time. Hardly anyone dares risk opposing venturesome new proposals for fear of being thought over-conservative.

Fad and Fallacy

The effect of this electric atmosphere on the financial executive is worth examining. There is no doubt that, taken as a whole, he is changing in response to the world around him. How? For the better? Is he moving in a progressive forward course or is he merely in orbit in a new cycle that is

---

†Reprinted from the *Financial Executive*, October 1968, pp. 12, 16, 20, 22, 24, 26, 30-32, copyright 1968, with permission of the Financial Executives Institute, 10 Madison Avenue, P.O. Box 1938, Morristown, NJ 07962-1938. (201) 898-4600.

really as ancient as recorded history? What is his metamorphosis in this accelerating century, now two-thirds gone and apparently headed for more whirlwinds in its final period? What is happening to the financial executive?

In attacking this alluring question, I would like to examine one or two premises—which I prefer to call fallacies—which seem to have been adopted by a great part of the management fraternity.

'Everything is Changing' Fallacy

The first and perhaps most basic of the fallacies besetting us today is that "everything is changing." Nothing, says this theory, is stable any more. The waves of obsolescence are washing away all of our foundations. Typical of current catch-phrases is "We have to run fast just to stand still." The implication is that the financial executive, like his fellows in management, is breathing a new atmosphere, in which little that he has previously learned is of value to him—that in order to qualify for today's race he must undergo radical transformation of his education, his reasoning processes, and his fundamental responses.

As background for an approach to this dilemma, let us reflect for a moment. Radical as today's changes are, they are perhaps not more so than those which have occurred in various periods of history. The perspective afforded by the past may surprise us with the reminder that other times and other men have been similarly burdened with the pressures of awesome change.

Dr. Emmanuel G. Mesthene, executive director of Harvard University's Program on Technology and Society, made the following comment in a talk at the American Management Association's Second International Conference: "It is difficult to identify what is significantly new about our age. People say it is an age of change. But there has never been an age that didn't change. Ah yes, they say, but our age changes faster than past ages. But the intellectual instruments and criteria of measurement that could tell us so do not exist.... Other people say that it is our technology that is new about our age. But there have been major technological innovations throughout history. It would be difficult to argue that the atomic bomb and the computer introduce more novelty in our time than gunpower and the printing press did in theirs."

Dr. Mesthene then thoughtfully acknowledges one phase of our current thinking that distinguishes it from the past—the sharpened awareness of change and of the implications of science and technology, and the fact that, as a society, we are probably concerned more deeply and more thoughtfully with the future than any previous generation. It is this characteristic of our age that brings us face to face with the subject of this article.

Perhaps we can glean from all of this a conclusion of some value to us in building a philosophical fortress against the turbulence of the day, as well as a base for attack on the problems which loom ahead. Perhaps we need to

146

recognize once more, in all its stark simplicity, the axiom that methods change but principles do not.

Principles Endure

Let us first freely admit that today's financial executive does exist in an age of lightning technological advance; that science is recreating his world of products, placing many of them farther outside his intellectual grasp than ever before; and that he directly suffers from the need to cope with the dazzling new face of the computer.

But is *everything* changing? I think we can point to some pretty basic things that are not. When the free enterprise principle flowered into the so-called industrial revolution of the Eighteenth and early Nineteenth Centuries, large quantities of capital and manpower were brought together and the now familiar problems of management began to appear. Ultimately, the practice of management, as related to the utilization of money and men, took on some of the characteristics of a science. In the early Twentieth Century, some accountants had begun to turn their eyes to the future, and controllership was born.

The principles of planning and control have been stated and elaborated many times. They have been developed into their present form largely under the cultivation of Financial Executives Institute during its 36 years of existence. For a long time they have been presented to the world, without material changes, as the proper functions of controllership. In recent years, treasurership has come within the scope of the Institute's interest, and an authoritative summary statement of this function is now published also. (See pages 159-160.)

It has long been recognized that the principles of control are more closely related to the social disciplines than to the mathematical. The interlock between human beings, highly trained in the techniques requisite to the conduct of today's business, is the essence of the control problem. This is strikingly clear at the points of organization contact in the classic triangle of supervision, embracing (1) a responsible manager, (2) the man to whom he is responsible, and (3) a staff control man. The planning process, the application of the budget principle, and the reporting relationship which emerges are purely results of disciplined individual responses. The science of this relationship has been expounded and refined. Its fundamentals have not changed since it was evolved, despite radical improvements in tools and methods.

Since principles do not change, we may identify here, quite intact, the guideposts for performance of financial executive functions. So long as business units live in an atmosphere of free enterprise—to whatever degree circumscribed by governmental interference—we will have the unchanging laws of business organization underlying the practice of financial executiveship.

Computer Revolution Fallacy

If the word "revolution" has not already been too much weakened by over-use, we may legitimately refer to what is going on in the world of data processing, communication, and recording as a computer revolution. I need not dwell on the infinity of potential development that confronts us at this bewildering hour of technological breakthroughs. This is not an illusion, but a cold reality.

The fallacy is in its alleged effect on management science. It creeps into the conversation and the literature of the times in the form of wholly unwarranted—almost panicky—assumptions. From sources with enough intelligence to know better, we hear that the new generation of computers will cause a universal and rock-bottom recasting of organization structures. We have been told that middle management, as such, is on its way out, or at least will be severely cut back because of the decision-making capacities of computers. We hear that most of the decentralization of the past few decades will be outmoded and that the "total" concept of data handling systems will bring about a massive recentralization of industrial operations. Finally, we hear that the new systems will render obsolete large numbers of the country's experienced executive manpower, and will demand the development of a wholly new breed of operating executive.

Extravagant Conjectures

There is a grain of the plausible in each of these propositions—just enough, I suppose, to lend it a touch of credibility. In each, too, there is enough appeal to the imagination to arouse us, and enough of the ring of prophecy to make us heed what just might be an important warning signal. The danger lies in the literal acceptance of these extravagant conjectures, and in allowing them to color our attitudes and sometimes to paralyze action.

As long as we are in the business of providing products which will be competitive in a selective, sometimes fickle, market, consisting of people who buy independently, we will have decisions to make. They will be production decisions, research and development decisions, marketing decisions. The point of operating decision is peculiarly the focal point of the financial executive's world, for where a decision is being made, there he, or a member of his staff, must be.

The basic decisions concerning what to produce, where and how to sell it, what development areas to pursue for improvement of product line, will remain with us forever. The very presence of these elements will continue, as now, to create a functionally departmentalized organization structure. We will always decentralize, so long as we can delegate. Whenever profit responsibility can be moved one step down the organization ladder we will send accountability with it. Whether computers are ultimately spread about the country like typewriters, or whether we finally all share the time of a single multi-billion dollar computer complex installed deep in the Colorado mountains makes not a particle of difference. Decentralization of profit-making and decision-making will persist because it is sound in principle; and the control tools provided by inspired controllership will be present as well.

Computers and Decision Making

How, then, will the computer revolution change the financial executive? Certainly it is accelerating the pace at which information is produced. By the same token it is stepping up the tempo at which both operating and staff thinking is brought to bear upon the decision point. As the man who has a strong hand in coordinating planning, leading into paths of control, the financial executive is equipped well or poorly to perform this task, depending upon the effectiveness of his information system.

He also finds himself in the vortex of a controversy concerning assignment of the procedures and data processing functions. It is not my view that these activities should, as has been proposed, be the duty of a new vice president. The financial executive at the vice presidential level appears to be best suited to handle this vital management tool.

Nor do I consider the use of the word "planning" in this limited sense appropriate to such an executive position. The planning function relates to the larger sphere of future product development, allocation of manpower and capital resources, facilities, growth rate, acquisitions, and so on. Data handling, like production planning, is a method rather than an end in itself—and as such is a problem of internal administration, regardless of how intricate it may become.

The question of assignment of the third generation computer system has raised a storm of conflicting opinion. Since its ancestors back to great-grandfather—punched card tabulating—have lived in the finance department, it is reluctant to move. Casting up all of the arguments, I feel that it belongs there as a tool broadly equivalent in importance to accounting science, budgetary practice, and the techniques of cost control. The responsibility for the provision of business information tends to attract the means for producing it.

Much criticism has been directed at controllers for adapting computer systems only to the volume processing of traditional accounting jobs and overlooking opportunities for its use as a part of a business information system for an entire company. These claims may be valid to some extent, but hardly justify upsetting the natural organization arrangement by transferring the computer to another department. Rather they suggest a new look at controllers by controllers to see if they are in fact fulfilling the management opportunities which are theirs.

They should find themselves as much concerned with production and inventory data, orders received data, and personnel statistics as they are with payrolls, cost distribution, and expense details—not just as producers of these figures but as users of them. When they have fulfilled their mission to bring to bear on each operating decision the optimum of interpreted information, they will have absorbed the so-called computer revolution and the computer as well.

"Money Man" vs. "Judgment Man"

One of the most subtle and costly illusions prevalent in business management is that the financial executive lives in a separate money world of his own, and that financial considerations in business decision making are something to be distinguished from other judgment factors. It begins with the assumption that the financial executive is not very much interested in ideas, but that his mental focus is fixed on the dollar sign. It takes form in a common misconception that policy and corporate planning are of concern to the financial staff only at a hypothetical point in the development of a plan at which quantification begins.

Not only does this fallacious tendency restrict the controller or treasurer in his range of contribution, but it correspondingly deprives operating and top management of the more mature thinking of which he is capable. Moreover it leads to the complementary notion that, since the financial executive is in all respects a money specialist, he has a monopoly on all considerations relating to money. This tends to place the operating executive (whether in production, sales, or general management) in an unreal world in which he deals with men, products, facilities, and plans, but feels he is in forbidden territory whenever dollars are mentioned.

Sea of Dollars

I do not mean to imply by this statement—obviously an exaggeration—that operating executives as a group are that naive. Yet the fallacy insidiously takes its toll. Reality says that the business, and each segment of it, floats on a sea of dollars. Every element of manpower, materials, production science, and marketing strategy has a statistical reflection and the ultimate common denominator is money. Unfortunately there is a latent fear of money and its complexities entertained by so-called non-financial people, which leads them to build a mental wall between it and them. Perhaps we have compounded this problem by failing to simplify the subject.

I prefer another approach, however. In my view, of all the varied contributions and services the financial executive supplies to his company, the ultimate is sound and objective business judgment. If we take a moment to imagine the birth of a new business venture, we might logically visualize asking one man to plan and design the product; another to provide it, whether by manufacture or purchase; and a third to get it into the hands of a customer in quantities and at prices which will furnish the income with which to do all of these things. The top, directing, and coordinating leadership for this triad of specialists is provided by a man whom we will call president, but he in turn finds that something more is needed. The missing ingredient is independent, objective judgment, supported by a professional information-gathering system. The financial man has entered the scene.

Over the years, we have seen this man propelled into prominence by the existence of a raw craving for objectivity and mature judgment, unhampered by the weight of operating responsibility. This is far from the accepted view that each organization needs a financial man to handle the record-keeping and reporting, to maintain a budget system, to get and manage capital, and so on. These important demands must be fulfilled too, but the business judgment factor, perhaps last to be recognized, is the dominant characteristic of the profession.

Business Judgment Factor

This quality, moreover, adheres to all levels of the organization line. Every operating manager has need of staff objectivity. The broadest and most acute need, of course, is in the president's office, but his dependence on a financial vice president or controller has its lesser counterpart in the demands made by a divisional general manager upon a divisional controller and by a manufacturing executive on the cost accounting manager.

The manner in which this very special value is delivered is familiar to all. The basic tools are accounting and budgeting techniques, a tailored structure of intelligent reporting, an experienced analytical function. From there, these merge into the higher realm of judgment—objective, informed, impartial, and ethical. At this point we can dispose of the fallacy that the financial executive is concerned only with dollar signs, along with the twin error that he is the only executive vitally concerned with money. All competent executives deal unceasingly with money and with figures, for in one sense this is the "name of the game." Further, the financial executive who runs true to his fine heritage is actually not just a "money man" but more accurately a "judgment man."

The issue I would like to discuss next never fails to stimulate cries of protest regardless of the way in which it is presented.

One Financial Executive or Two

I am referring to the trend in the organization of industrial companies toward providing a single top financial executive. Many years ago this was common practice among corporations, the treasurer being the executive fully responsible for all financial affairs. It is probably a fairly safe generalization to say that when controllers began to emerge as such they usually reported to treasurers. Little by little this changed and many controllers found their way into the top organization row where, alongside treasurers, they reported to presidents or other chief executive officers.

In this decade the wheel seems to be turning again, and there is a growing tendency to re-establish the single top financial executive. Frequently he is titled vice president-finance and may have reporting to him both a controller and a treasurer. There is a wide diversity of titles and reporting arrangements, however, and predominant patterns are difficult to identify. We must also be cautious about assuming that the current trend—conspicuous though it is—has become dominant.

The trend in organization thinking which I have described is of paramount importance to financial executives. It affects their composite performance, opportunity, and image. It probably derives mostly from chief operating executives' instinctive desire to center all financial problems in one staff unit rather than to divide the assignment between two men and cope with the problem of keeping both informed and remembering which financial question should be referred to each. There is no doubt that combining all so-called financial functions under one staff executive simplifies the top executive's job—at least theoretically—but there is serious question whether he can afford the cost of such convenience in terms of congestion in the flow of financial staff work.

It is my view that the supposed advantage of uniting the controllership and treasurership responsibilities under one man may be a costly illusion. Let me elaborate a little by means of a brief review of these two functions, which, by custom and practice, are generally accepted as identifiable subdivisions of the work of financial executives.

CONTROLLERSHIP

Controllership is that staff function which maintains a system of control and measurement of the operation of the business. The word control is, of course, used in a very special sense and leaves decisions, vetoes, discipline, and all the various other executive prerogatives to line management.

The controller reserves the right to insist, however, that systematic planning be done for the application of control techniques; that the organization be structured to assign defined areas of income and spending; that the control feature be exercised by means of interpretive reporting provided by the controller and his staff; and that he be given full responsibility for accounting and for the coordination of budget activity.

It is clear that to carry out this assignment a controller must be conversant with every significant detail of the operation of the business. He must acquire intimate knowledge of its products, pricing, markets, manufacturing—every aspect, in fact, which is the concern of the president or chief executive officer. Only then can he apply the measurement and control practices which keep his business on its course.

It is not my purpose to go over old ground by elaborating on the accepted functions of controllership. I do, however, want to call attention to certain collateral demands which cannot be avoided.

It is commonly accepted that the controller personally must be well versed in all areas of federal and local taxation, for the tax problem is always present in business decision making and all of management must look to the controller for guidance. It is also his responsibility to study the techniques and economics of data processing and communication equipment at least deeply enough to use it to best advantage, if not to coordinate its application company-wide.

Further, the exercise of the measurement and appraisal function makes mandatory an understanding of external economic and social forces. These bear directly on the appraisal of the sales forecast or budget and other operating plans. Add to these certain demands which fall on the corporate chief accounting officer—the need to represent the company in its relationships with governmental agencies and frequently to speak for it in the financial and accounting phases of negotiations with labor unions, dealers, large contract suppliers, and so on—and it becomes evident that a position of very high calibre has emerged in the corporate scene.

Controller's Contribution

But we have not yet seen the apex of the contribution which the controller is in a position to make and which he does make when expected and permitted to do so by top management. The controller should be the most profit-conscious executive in the company and should apply this profit-sense in hundreds upon hundreds of ways. In his particular staff status he can turn the profit spotlight relentlessly on every angle of the business, every proposal, every area of planning.

In this category come such opportunities as the design and coordination of cost-control programs; the utilization of improved equipment and procedures throughout the company's complex of paperwork; the constructive scrutiny of proposals to enter new markets or to reduce prices; the protective warning against inflated sales budgets as a justification for inflated spending. Here too fall the uncovering of unprofitable products, the excision of waste, the recasting of expense account policy. A thousand little savings and a few big ones can make the difference between a handsome net earning and a mediocre one.

I need not add that the point of location from which the controller can operate most effectively is that place on the organization chart from which he can make his thoughts known directly to the chief operating executive and can express them with authority to all others at the highest level. The true controller should report directly to the president.

TREASURERSHIP

I would like to turn to the other side of the financial executive's domain—treasurership. The heart of this function is the procurement and use of capital. His career is centered in the sources, input, and commitment of money, and especially on the return its skillful handling yields.

The treasurer is in theory something more of an operating man and less a staff man than the controller. In a sense, it might be said that the treasurer operates with money as the production manager operates with materials, machines, and men.

The treasurer is the guardian of capital raising activities. He is the architect of the company's capital structure. He maintains borrowing sources, both long- and short-term, and conducts a complex relationship with an army of competitive bankers. He worries about maintaining an active market for the company's stock; about its public image in Wall Street; and about the impressions being carried away by the visiting investment analysts. When a security issue is imminent, he carefully weighs the avenues open and shapes his recommendations with a view to net cost, debt ratio, maturities, tax effect, and so on.

The treasurer also accepts a heavy duty in the investment of funds. The granting of credit alone is a trust of magnitude, particularly in the present period of general credit deterioration. And the investment of excess cash has opened up new vistas in the past few years of the profit squeeze. He is concerned with installment selling (sometimes through a separate finance subsidiary), leasing, foreign exchange, and all the tricks of the money trade, which must be sifted, selected, and used with skill and discretion in the conduct of a profitable financial operation. He is today very often involved in investment of pension funds, sometimes even supervising the company portfolio.

Treasurer's Orbit

Like the controller, he is a student of economics, but with a little more emphasis on money rates, governmental fiscal policy here and in other countries, and the stock market. He lives with the duty of providing capital for his company on favorable terms, and his favorite nightmare is a sharp rise in bond prices just after he has completed a large refunding operation.

154

It is clear that the treasurer moves in an orbit requiring authority to deal with the financial fraternity. He also needs access to top management and even, on occasion, to the Board of Directors, of which he is often a member. His continuous concern is the solution of major problems of financial planning and the design of ways to make the company's money work profitably, with due consideration or risk factors. For these reasons it is difficult to place the mature treasurer in any position lower than the organization line reporting to the president. Like the controller, he must be there to be effective.

I have tried to describe briefly two recognized and distinct staff functions, each requiring personal competency, special training, major executive responsibility, and proximity to the top of the chain of command. This picture is not as valid, of course, in small companies or in decentralized operations not having full treasury functions. In the normal corporate entity of medium or large size, however, the separation of duties endows the president with a more powerful force for control, since the controller, acting as his arm in that field, is free of the array of major time-consuming tasks which demand the time of a treasurer and which cannot be delegated.

The number and variety of activities which these functions involve—the many conferences demanding the presence of a financial officer who must prepare himself in advance; discussions with the president, with other company executives, with directors, shareholders, bankers, attorneys, public accountants, underwriters, insurers, consultants, government officials, and sundry others who cannot be content unless they confer with the man with the title; not to mention the very considerable task of selecting and directing a staff organization in the gathering, analysis, and presentation of information—these warn of a paralyzing congestion if one man undertakes them all. The logical solution would seem to lie in the assignment of two men to do two jobs.

Changing Profit Motive

If the typical financial executive is really changing, perhaps the way to locate and identify the change that is taking place is to examine his underlying attitudes. To begin with, his fidelity to the profit motive has never been questioned. The word "financial" itself is so allied to the word "profit" in the public mind that financial executives are nearly everywhere assumed, even by the uninitiated, to be exerting on their companies a strong pull in the direction of maximum profit.

Perhaps in this age of change something is happening to the profit motive itself. Certainly it has had more apologists and more interpretations than any other industrial doctrine. I have even noted a defiant wave of cynicism in recent years, based on a theory of action purely in self-interest. I have, on the other hand, been conscious of widespread protestations from industrial leaders of the philanthropic responsibility of business and a growing willingness to satisfy it. Enlightenment comes slowly, but on the subject of profits we need that fine balance that makes identical the interests of management, employees, customers, and owners.

In the sometimes foggy atmosphere surrounding a discussion of this subject, Peter F. Drucker contributes a breath of fresh air in his book, *The Practice of Management* (New York: Harper & Row, 1954). He says:

> The average businessman when asked what a business is, is likely to answer: 'An organization to make a profit.' And the average economist is likely to give the same answer. But this answer is not only false; it is irrelevant....
>
> This does not mean that profit and profitability are unimportant. It does mean that profitability is not the purpose of business enterprise and business activity, but a limiting factor on it. Profit is not the explanation, cause or rationale of business behavior and business decisions, but the test of their validity....
>
> If we want to know what a business is we have to start with its purpose.... There is only one valid definition of business purpose: to create a customer....
>
> Because it is its purpose to create a customer, any business enterprise has two—and only these two—basic functions: marketing and innovation. They are the entrepreneurial functions....
>
> To emphasize only profit ... misdirects managers to the point where they may endanger the survival of the business. To obtain profit today they tend to undermine the future.... (pp. 35, 37, 62)

These words deserve the thoughtful consideration of financial executives. They lead to deep self-searching questions concerning how each can make his best contribution to marketing and innovation. They cause him to reassess his scale of values, to inquire if his criteria have been sound and his appraisal formulae valid.

It seems possible that we are seeing the gradual substitution of a progress motive for the profit motive. If this is true, then corporate profit, indispensable as it is, takes its place as only one of the impelling forces of business rather than the primary one. Investment analysts, and even the investing public, have long since discovered that the 10-year comparative balance sheet and income statement do not begin to reveal the health and promise of a company. It is up to the financial executive to find those elements that are vital to progress, weigh them, and point out the opportunities they offer.

In this connection I want to call your attention to a pronouncement of Financial Executives Institute contained in the officially authorized statement of the controller's functions on pages 159-160. It has been there, in almost identical form, for almost 20 years, although few controllers profess to live up to it. It says that it is one of the functions of controllership "To consult with all segments of management responsible for policy or action concerning any phase of the operation of the business as it relates to the attainment of objectives and the effectiveness of policies, organization, and procedures."

A broad statement? Yes, undoubtedly, and probably little known and seldom really understood. But not too broad, in my opinion, for it releases the financial executive from the strictures of statistics and opens the door to achievement. "... any phase of the business ... attainment of objectives ... effectiveness of policies...." Granted that the freedom to address top management in this language is reserved only for those financial executives who earn it, we are nevertheless shown here the ultimate of the function of appraisal and measurement. We have here the "judgment man" at his best. We have the epitomization of the "progress motive" superseding the limitations of pure "profit motive."

CONCLUSION

When all has been said that can be said today, and we have peered into tomorrow as far as our vision will allow, what is really changing about the financial executive? I can do little better than to observe that he is growing. He is more surely than ever before a part of management decision and policy. We are already seeing in quantity what was a lone prototype only a few years ago—the man of judgment, whose counsel is now sought not just because he controls the accounting department and the business information system, but because he is an intelligent student of business and identifies himself with its practice at the highest level of responsibility.

We have prophesied this development; we now begin to see it manifest. The tempo of business accelerates, technology rushes toward us headlong, and we become steadily more conscious of orientation to the social and governmental structure of these disturbing days. Even international business, no longer distant, begins to color our daily work with new complexities. I consider it neither trite nor an exaggeration to say that the financial executive is changing by growing—perhaps in part because I tend to view him in the background of man's unlimited capacity to grow.

Declining Influence?

I was much interested in the article by Professor Gordon Donaldson, of the Harvard Business School, published in the April 1967 issue of *Financial Executive*. In it he argued that the influence of financial executives will gradually decline. He based this conclusion on the growing supply of capital—particularly capital internally generated—and the diminishing emphasis on capital procurement as compared, for example, with manpower or facilities development.

I cannot accept such reasoning, but I am grateful to its author for spurring me to follow through to the opposite conclusion. I believe that the premise of growing capital resources and declining opportunity for its use is false. It also seems to me that the problem of sources and profitable use of capital could hardly diminish even if the balance between demand and supply were to shift over the long term. The effective use of capital, the earning of an appropriate return on it, and the relationships of the various elements having claims on the resources of a business—shareholders, lenders, employees, executives, and so on—will always demand objective financial thinking of the highest order.

Controllership and Treasurership Functions Defined By FEI

The first official statement of the responsibilities of the corporate treasurership function was approved in 1962 by the Board of Directors of Financial Executives Institute (established in 1931 as Controllers Institute of America). For many years the Institute and its predecessor body had published an established list of functions of controllership. The newly approved list of treasurership functions was developed coincident with the change of scope and name of the Institute from Controllers Institute to Financial Executives Institute.

FINANCIAL MANAGEMENT

CONTROLLERSHIP

Planning for Control
To establish, coordinate and administer, as an integral part of management, an adequate plan for the control of operations. Such a plan would provide, to the extent required in the business, profit planning, programs for capital investing and for financing, sales forecasts, expense budgets and cost standards, together with the necessary procedures to effectuate the plan.

Reporting and Interpreting
To compare performance with operating plans and standards, and to report and interpret the results of operations to all levels of management and to the owners of the business. This function includes the formulation of accounting policy, the coordination of systems and procedures, the preparation of operating data and of special reports as required.

TREASURERSHIP

Provision of Capital
To establish and execute programs for the provision of the capital required by the business, including negotiating the procurement of capital and maintaining the required financial arrangements.

Investor Relations
To establish and maintain an adequate market for the company's securities and, in connection therewith, to maintain adequate liaison with investment bankers, financial analysts and shareholders.

Short-Term Financing
To maintain adequate sources for the company's current borrowings from commercial banks and other lending institutions.

Evaluating and Consulting

To consult with all segments of management responsible for policy or action concerning any phase of the operation of the business as it relates to the attainment of objectives and the effectiveness of policies, organization structure and procedures.

Tax Administration

To establish and administer tax policies and procedures.

Government Reporting

To supervise or coordinate the preparation of reports to government agencies.

Protection of Assets

To assure protection for the assets of the business through internal control, internal auditing and assuring proper insurance coverage.

Economic Appraisal

To continuously appraise economic and social forces and government influences, and to interpret their effect upon the business.

Banking and Custody

To maintain banking arrangements, to receive, have custody of and disburse the company's monies and securities and to be responsible for the financial aspects of real estate transactions.

Credits and Collections

To direct the granting of credit and the collection of accounts due the company, including the supervision of required special arrangements for financing sales, such as time payment and leasing plans.

Investments

To invest the company's funds as required, and to establish and coordinate policies for investment in pension and other similar trusts.

Insurance

To provide insurance coverage as may be required.

JAMES L. PEIRCE:
A BIBLIOGRAPHY

"The Controllership Function: A Modern Concept." *The Controller* 20 (September 1952): 419-422, 428, 430-432, 434.

"Controllership and Accounting: A Contrast." *The Canadian Chartered Accountant* 63 (July 1953): 5-16. *The Controller* 21 (September 1953): 410-412, 429-432.

"The Budget Comes of Age." *Harvard Business Review* 32 (May-June 1954): 58-66. Similar articles were published under the title "Budgets and People: A Positive Approach," in *Guides to Modern Financial Planning*, Financial Management Series Number 104 (Papers presented at the Finanical Management Conference, American Management Association, Hotel Roosevelt, New York, November 18-20, 1953), New York: American Management Association, 1953, 3-13, and under the title "A Positive Approach to Budgets and People," in *The Financial Manager's Job*, New York: American Management Association, 1964, 180-192.

"The Planning and Control Concept." *The Controller* 22 (September 1954): 403-406, 422, 424-425.

"What Makes a Budget Work." *Illinois Manufacturers' Costs Association Monthly Bulletin* (April 1955): 6 printed pages.

"Controllership Motivation." *The Controller* 23 (August 1955): 367-369, 396-399.

"Controllership and Cost Accounting." *The Controller* 24 (August 1956): 359-361, 384-386.

"Control by Budget." *The Controller* 25 (July 1957): 327-330, 352, 354, 356. *Business Budgeting* 6 (September 1957): 5-12.

"The New Image of Controllership." *Financial Executive* 31 (January 1963): 13-15, 19, 36, 38-39.

"Budgetary Accounting and Its Prospects." *Financial Executive* 36 (February 1968): 66-70, 72, 74.

"The Changing Financial Executive." *Financial Executive* 36 (October 1968): 12, 16, 20, 22, 24, 26, 30-32.

THE ACCOUNTING HALL OF FAME

THE Accounting Hall of Fame was established at The Ohio State University in 1950 for the purpose of honoring accountants who have made or are making significant contributions to the advancement of accounting since the beginning of the twentieth century. Through 1997, 60 leading accountants from the United States and other countries have been elected to the Hall of Fame.

While selection to the Hall of Fame is intended to honor the people so chosen, it is also intended to be a recognition of distinguished service contributions to the progress of accounting in any of its various fields. Evidence of such service includes contributions to accounting research and literature, significant service to professional accounting organizations, wide recognition as an authority in some field of accounting, advancement of accounting education, and public service. A member must have reached a position of eminence from which the nature of his or her contributions may be judged.

Elections to the Hall of Fame are made by a Board of Nominations consisting of up to 45 eminent accountants from each of the following three groups: public accountants, educators, and industrial and governmental accountants. Each Board member serves a fixed term. Starting in 1973, Board membership became international. In addition to members from the United States, the Board has included members from Australia, Canada, England, Japan, Mexico, and other countries.

Nomination and election to the Accounting Hall of Fame by the Board are made annually by mail in two steps. Individual members of the Board are asked to nominate a living or deceased accountant for possible election to the Hall of Fame. From these preliminary nominations, a ballot is prepared containing the names, alphabetically listed, of not more than four candidates who have been nominated most frequently. The members of the Board of Nominations then cast their votes for one of the four nominees. The candidate on the ballot receiving the most votes is elected to the Hall. In the event that several candidates receive the same number of votes, more than one candidate may be elected.

Evidence of election to the Accounting Hall of Fame takes three forms. A certificate issued under the seal of The Ohio State University and signed by the President of the University and a representative of the Board of Nominations is presented to each person elected (or to the person's representative when the person elected is deceased). The names of the elected persons are inscribed on a scroll, and a photographic portrait of each person elected together with the citation attesting to the election are permanently displayed in the corridors of the College of Business at The Ohio State University. The presentation of the certificate usually takes place at the annual meeting of the American Accounting Association. Members of The Ohio State University faculty are not eligible for election to the Accounting Hall of Fame.

THE ACCOUNTING HALL OF FAME
MEMBERSHIP

1950

George Oliver May

Robert Hiester Montgomery

William Andrew Paton

1951

Arthur Lowes Dickinson

Henry Rand Hatfield

1952

Elijah Watt Sells

Victor Hermann Stempf

1953

Arthur Edward Andersen

Thomas Coleman Andrews

Charles Ezra Sprague

Joseph Edmund Sterrett

1954

Carman George Blough

Samuel John Broad

Thomas Henry Sanders

Hiram Thompson Scovill

1955

Percival Flack Brundage

1956

Ananias Charles Littleton

1957

Roy Bernard Kester

Hermann Clinton Miller

1958
Harry Anson Finney
Arthur Bevins Foye
Donald Putnam Perry

1959
Marquis George Eaton

1960
Maurice Hubert Stans

1961
Eric Louis Kohler

1963
Andrew Barr
Lloyd Morey

1964
Paul Franklin Grady
Perry Empey Mason

1965
James Loring Peirce

1968
George Davis Bailey
John Lansing Carey
William Welling Werntz

1974
Robert Martin Trueblood

1975
Leonard Paul Spacek

1976
John William Queenan

1977
Howard Irwin Ross

166

1978
Robert Kuhn Mautz

1979
Maurice Moonitz

1980
Marshall Smith Armstrong

1981
Elmer Boyd Staats

1982
Herbert Elmer Miller

1983
Sidney Davidson

1984
Henry Alexander Benson

1985
Oscar Strand Gellein

1986
Robert Newton Anthony

1987
Philip Leroy Defliese

1988
Norton Moore Bedford

1989
Yuji Ijiri

1990
Charles Thomas Horngren

1991
Raymond John Chambers

1992
David Solomons

1993
Richard Thomas Baker

1994
Robert Thomas Sprouse

1995
William Wager Cooper

1996
William Henry Beaver
Charles Arthur Bowsher
Donald James Kirk

1997
Thomas Junior Burns
John Campbell Burton

THE ACCOUNTING HALL OF FAME: THOMAS J. BURNS SERIES IN ACCOUNTING HISTORY

Volume 1: Samuel J. Broad: A Collection of His Writings (1993)

Volume 2: T. Coleman Andrews: A Collection of His Writings (1996)

Volume 3: James L. Peirce: A Collection of His Writings (1997)